31 WAYS

of

INFLUENCE

Volume 2

31 WAYS

of

INFLUENCE

Volume 2

Compiled by Dr. Derashay Zorn

For information about special discounts for bulk purchase, contact the sales department at **sales@divine-order.org**

Designed by D' Technology

Published by:
D.O.R.M. International Publishing
A Christian Publisher located in Atlanta, Georgia (USA)
Visit our website at **www.derashay.com**
Printed in the United States of America
Second Volume: March 2021
10 9 8 7 6 5 4 3 2 1
Library of Congress Cataloging-in-Publication Data

Dr. Derashay Worthen-Zorn
31 Ways of Influence Volume 2./ Dr. Derashay Worthen-Zorn
ISBN-13: 978-0-9862493-4-1
ISBN-10: 0986249341

DEDICATION

This book is dedicated to every woman in the world. Our vision is to let you know that you are a Proverbs 31 Woman, tailor-made by God for such a time as this, to do good works within the earth. He has an unmeasurable love for you. By birthright, you are designed to be an influencer. Through this project, we stand with you to break every stereotype and disrupt societal inequality practices that have been placed upon you, which have formed a false identity. Collectively, we rise as the Daughters of Zion in purpose, power, permission, and prosperity. We know you are called to impact nations, and we couldn't setback another second without seeing you placed in your rightful position. We are calling forth the virtuous woman within you.

Know you are H.E.R!

You are virtuous.
You are that woman that the world needs to see shine.
You are a woman of noble character.
You are that woman who knows how to invest wisely.
You are fearfully and wonderfully made.
You are that woman with many entrepreneurship endeavors.
You are that woman who generates multiple streams of income.
You are that woman of confidence.
You are the woman whose voice is needed in the earth.
You are that woman with good merchandise.
You are that woman who cares for the needy.
You are that woman who children honor and praise.
You are that woman who knows how to conduct business affairs.
You are that woman of dignity.
You are that woman full of grace.
You are that woman who reverences God.
You are more than enough.

You are a Proverbs 31 Woman!

Get Your Free Resources

A comprehensive package of exclusive resources comes with this book as a free bonus. There's also a free online course designed to provide additional guidance. To be sure you get the most out of this book, download all the extras and access the companion course at the link below:

https://px.fyi/31WaysV2

ACKNOWLEDGMENTS

First and foremost, I give honor and thanks to God for trusting me with this book and every project associated with it. It has been such an honor to have my steps ordered by Him.

I want to express gratitude to my co-authors who caught the vision and ran with it. Your collaboration with this project made it unique and just what God ordered for His people. Each of your portions is vital to this journey as a vessel of God to empower, encourage, and educate women to fulfill their purpose. You are unique in the sight of God. Because of your obedience, He is going to enlarge the tent of your dwelling and expand your territory. It has been an honor to work with you.

I want to thank Denise Walker, founder and chief editor of Armor of Hope Writing Services, and the editing team for their commitment to making this project shine with a spirit of excellence.

I would also like to thank every individual who purchases this book. Your support and belief in this project is bringing it to life.

TABLE OF CONTENTS

31 WAYS

of

INFLUENCE

Compiled by Dr. Derashay Zorn

I AM H.E.R
Make The Time To Become

Dr. Derashay Zorn

Strength and honor are her clothing; She shall
rejoice in time to come.
Proverbs 31:25

When I look at the Proverbs 31 woman, I see a woman who was very wise with her time. Her ability to optimize her time, talent, and treasures reflected her seriousness of being a steward over what God had entrusted within her. We can all agree that as a wife, mother, serial preneur, investor, philanthropist, negotiator, employer, etc. She handled her responsibilities well. The picture of her looks perfect, but I am sure there were many challenges in her life. However, she didn't waste her time focusing on the challenges. I see a woman who leveraged the time she had to complete her dreams, visions, and aspiration so that she could influence and impact her family, city, regions, and nations while making a sustainable income.

Some would say it's not realistic to be a Proverbs 31 woman as they look at how she manages what she was given and say it's impossible. I would say this would be true for the imposter. Otherwise, I challenge their thoughts. God would not give us visions and dreams if He didn't entrust us to manage them and haven't equipped us to fulfill them. When trying to copy the things others do, we will never be effective in achieving the same results. Many women fail because we are trying to be carbon copies of someone else instead of being our authentic selves. This is where the struggle happens because we try to do things that we were not called and not anointed to do. If you are not called to sew, build websites, edit books, be a travel agent, or sell things that don't align with your purpose, ask yourself why are you trying to do it? It's not about copying what she did, but it's about walking in the godly character that she displayed.

It was her character that produced her success personally, professionally, and spiritually. That's what's going to be necessary to do everything God has ordained for our lives. We must operate in our own lane. I'm sure many women were doing things based upon cultural norms, religious practices, or just their way. However, she didn't allow that to hinder what God needed to manifest in her life. I believe she was very focused on her vision and purpose and chose not to be distracted by anything else. This is why the scripture mentions she excelled them all.

She was a woman with a vision that understood there was no time for idleness if she was going to accomplish it. I am convinced that she was very strategic with her time and she lived a calendared life. Therefore, she made intentional usage of time to work toward her vision. She was not one of those who was trying to find the time to implement what God had given her, neither did she waste time doing things that were not a part of God's plan for her life. She understood that putting in the work now would bring forth the fruit in its appointed time.

One day I made the time to become HER

Once upon a time, I lived in a world of false belief, where I thought I didn't have the time to pursue my dreams, goals, and passion. There was no way I could be a Proverbs 31 woman. I developed this false belief due to becoming a parent before what I considered its appropriate time. When I initially entered parenthood, it took me down a road that halted everything in my life as I became consumed with it. At that moment, I didn't have the time to be educated, employed, or become an entrepreneur. To be honest, I wasn't sure if living out my dreams was still possible. I later in life found out I was so wrong. I wasted a lot of time living in a false reality. My limiting beliefs were hindering me from becoming everything that God had chosen for me. These beliefs had to be broken if I was going to fulfill my dreams, become an influencer, and impact my family, city, regions, and the world while making a sustainable income. This journey has not always been comfortable, but it's been worth it.

MAKE THE TIME TO BECOME H.E.R
-DR. DERASHAY ZORN

As a little girl, I always had big dreams and a plan for my life. In my plans, I would finish high school and college, stay pure until marriage, become a computer programmer analyst technician, have children, buy a beautiful house in a good neighborhood, have a nice car, have a lot of money, be able to take care of my grandma, and live happily ever after, in that exact order. There was a determination inside of me not to become another statistic and a product of my chaotic childhood environment. However, all of it caught up with me and temporarily, I was caught up in its vicious cycle.

At the age of 16, I entered parenthood as I delivered my first son. I was just a child myself who had newly acquired adult responsibilities. This life event took me on the road of readjusting and rethinking my life plans. I thought, "Okay, the 5th item on my list came first, but I can still fulfill my dreams with some adjustments." Everything seemed durable at first because I couldn't calculate the blind spot that awaited me on this journey. Due to unfortunate circumstances, I had to drop out of school. This wasn't a part of the readjustment, but it became my reality.

As I became an at-home mom, the events that had taken place begin to discourage me and alter my optimistic thinking. I begin to doubt the possibilities of my childhood dreams becoming true. Society labels and my childhood environment factors formed my beliefs as aspects of my life unfolded the exact ways I told myself I would not become. I was officially a high school dropout, an unwed mother, jobless, and living with a boyfriend. This was familiar within my family environment. So, I began to negotiate with facts and determined it was all over. As time went by, I gave up on the plan and found myself at the age of 21 with three children and no progression in any other area of my life. I had allowed my emotions to shift and my attitude to just go with the flow.

One day I woke up with a heavy heart as I looked at the boys and grieved because I knew that I could not provide the best life for them. Their father was awesome at providing for us and being there for them. Also, what would be our fate if something happened to him? He could die, lose his job, become unable to work, or decide to leave. Then, what? However, I knew they could have more if I dared to pursue my dreams. At this point, I didn't believe it was possible, neither did I believe I had the capacity to achieve it. So much time had gone by, and I had only completed the eighth grade. Then, I had more responsibilities with the boys. Where would I find the time to pursue anything?

Even though I knew something had to change, I wanted to lead by example so the boys would not fall within the same cycle on both sides of our family from generation to generation. With my now formed belief that I could do it, I found my boyfriend encouraging me to go after it. I remember crying out to God about why He kept giving me these babies, and I was not in a place to help. I wanted them to become productive citizens, educated, and influencers for the Kingdom of God. But I knew there were somethings I needed to do to support the desire. It became my fuel that ignited the fire of my faith.

I found strength in Jesus, to do what I thought was impossible. I obtained my GED after three attempts. Then, I decided I wanted to attempt to pursue a college education. There were a few things I had to work out if I was going to take on this challenge. This was the first time in my life where I had to learn how to modify my activities where I could take care of the children and do what was required for me to grow and develop. I began to evaluate my schedule by looking at how I utilized the 24 hours

God had given me. I had to determine first where I would find the time. It just appeared that I did not have time to fit school into my busy schedule. As I pondered, the light bulb went off. Since I was a stay at home mom, scheduling my class would be easy. All I needed to do was select courses centered around the time the boys were in school. That was a great idea as it wouldn't require a babysitter. However, there was a serious matter I needed to figure out. My youngest son was not of school age, and we could not afford what they were asking for daycare.

Therefore, I thought I would just take him to school with me. We could sit in the class with my other sons, so why not have him sit in class with me? Of course, you know this was against school policy. But I was not going to allow it to deter me. Once I enrolled in school, I found some other moms whose situations were like mines. We came together, supported one another, and agreed that we would take turns watching the kids on campus throughout the day. We made our class schedules together so that one person would always be available to watch the children. Now that school hours and childcare were taken care of, I was on my way.

As I entered college to earn a diploma in computer programing, I quickly learned I had to play catch up on all I missed from high school. This would require my studies to be longer than the average student since I had to fill in the missing pieces while successfully acquiring what was needed to pass my courses. Because I wanted this, it was time to make positive adjustments in my mind, attitude, and behaviors that would set me up for success and enhance my family's prosperity. I had to come up with a plan on how I was going to do it. I evaluated my schedule and asked myself some real questions. I asked myself what value I was getting by visiting my grandmother's house every day. I started to look at precisely the type of activities we were doing over there. How much time was I spending over there? I then weighed it all on how it would successfully impact or influence my educational endeavor. I discovered that I had more time than I thought.

BE INTENTIONAL WITH YOUR TIME
-DR. DERASHAY ZORN

Even though it was my grandmother's house, and it was everyone's routine to meet up there, I needed to make some hard decisions. I had to become more productive with the time I've been given. I loved visiting her, meeting up with my sisters, cousins, and nephews, joking and playing around with the family. This was our way of staying in touch with one another. However, the amount of time I was putting in over there each week could be optimized by redirecting it toward my study time. I played around and tried splitting the time in half, but it didn't work in my favor. So, I eventually stop going over every day because

I wanted to focus on my education. I was talked about and mocked for doing it, but I know it was the right choice when I looked at reality.

As I matriculated through school and reached for higher degrees, as I was finishing up my associate degree, my boyfriend and I got married. We finally stopped living in sin and got our life in order before God. Also, we found ourselves going back to church and giving our life to the Lord. I decided I would not stop my education endeavors, so I pursued a BS in Computer Information System. It would have positioned me to get an excellent job and decent pay. Soon after that, I was called into the ministry. This was another significant adjustment in my life. Now, I had to balance home, children, ministry, and school. I found myself again having to prioritize my time. It's amazing what you will find when you take a moment and analyze how your time is utilized.

In this season of my life, the boys were a little older. They didn't require as much attention, and it gave me a bit of flexibility with my time. I reevaluated my time and figured out how I could optimize and maximize it. I realized the boys were a lot more independent when it came to their homework. I could just go over the instructions, see if they needed an example, and they were off. In the meantime, while they were getting homework in, I could do homework for myself that didn't require a lot of focus so I could be available in the event they needed me. Then, I would do the rest of my work later.

This is where the challenge really came with managing time. Everything was going well until I finished school and entered the workforce. Then, one year later, I launched my first business and pursued a Master of Science in Information System Management. When I started my entrepreneurship endeavor, I did not leave my job. Time management became very crucial as God began to enlarge my territory. By this time, I had a child in middle school and two in elementary. In addition, we had to divide the time with the youngest child who desired to play football. It was the first time we experience our children wanting to do sports because they were very intellectual. Boy, did it stretch me with time, and I had to get creative with how I utilized every second of it.

My baby started something different in the household with his football adventure. This would cause my oldest son to venture off into tennis. This game was a little different, and it didn't require as much as football. After the football experience, it made this a bit easier with managing our time.

Because I specialized in computer programming and database management, the course work needed to be done without interruptions. The only time this was possible in my house was when everyone was asleep. It caused me to adopt a new sleeping pattern where I would wake up in the middle of the night to get my homework done and study the Bible. I began living a calendared life to optimize my time to get the most out of my day. I incorporated my kids and husband into my learning experience. We started drive time university, where the kids would quiz me on my work for the week. Of course, I would have everything laid out, so they knew what to ask. Also, I would take that time to do spelling and math quizzes for them. It's all about preparation.

For me, things gradually were placed on my plate one at a time, and I had to learn how to balance it all without allowing anything to fall over and left undone. With this, I became very meticulous about how I spent my time and how others used it. I learned the fundamental principles through Ecclesiastic 3:1, "To everything there is a season, A time for every purpose under heaven." This became vital as I begin to walk it out and prioritize my life. I still use these principles to this day. I utilize these to run four active businesses, a ministry, an online bible college, host three radio shows a week, and travel for the work of the ministry. The time has come where I can rejoice in the manifestation of God's word for my life. Where I am today was not built overnight, and I can rejoice in my now. However, I am continuously putting my hand to work because I know there's more to come.

Be Intentional with your time

I had to become intentional with my time like the Proverbs 31 woman. I had to examine and prioritize it so I could create the life I desired. We must be intentional with the time God gives us if we are ever going to produce the fruit of His word. Therefore, I had to define my priorities and assign them to the time given to me.

Do not omit the team

Players on the team are critical to your success in becoming everything that God has chosen for your life. God has

DO NOT OMIT THE TEAM
-DR. DERASHAY ZORN

provided others to help us on the journey. Everyone on the team has an important role, whether they are internal or external team players. You must know their roles and position so that your expectations are not beyond their qualification for your life. It's also vital that you leverage and not leave out the home team as you are pursuing God's word for your life. Take advantage of what they can bring to the table and how it can push you into your destiny. We can't forget or leave out our team of experts and the wise counsel who are part of your winning circle. Identify who they are so they can equip you through their experience and expertise. The team accelerates your growth and the completion of your endeavors.

SUPPLICATION

Dear God,

Thank you for your faithfulness in ensuring that your word will not come back to you void but accomplish what you have sent it to do in my life. In the name of Jesus, I thank you for the strength and wisdom to make the time for my visions and dreams. Give me the peace and comfort in understanding that it is okay to take time for me without feeling as if I have neglected others. I thank you for maturing me in my faith that I will no longer be negligent with my purpose because I understand the negative impact on my life and others' lives. I cast down every vain imagination that has poof itself up against your word.

Today, I choose to take the time to focus on your plan for my life. I thank you for the wisdom to balance everything you have given so that nothing will go unattended in the name of Jesus. It is your word that is the lamp upon my feet and the light upon my path that shall guide me to move in the right season, at the right time. Glory to your Holy Name! I declare, in the name of Jesus, I will no longer be hidden, under exposed, or apologetic by choosing to devote the time needed to fulfill my purpose. As you have written, I am a city on a hill that cannot be hidden.

Thank you, Lord, for breaking old habits that have hindered my success in the name of Jesus. I am a new creation in Christ Jesus with a renewed attitude within my mind, heart, and soul. I bless your name because there is nothing I cannot do. I thank you that everything I touch shall prosper and my faith will be magnified in my works. I honor you for being a living sacrifice that is holy and acceptable unto you. Unto you, I give all the glory and praise. It's in the majestic name of Jesus that I have prayed. Amen.

AFFIRMATION

- I will dedicate time to pursue my purpose.

- I will prioritize my activities.

- I will focus on my dreams, goals, and aspirations.

- I will give myself the care needed to become what God has chosen in my life.

- I can achieve anything I put my mind too.

- I shall conquer anything that hinders me from finishing my goals.

- I shall eliminate distractions.

- I shall be wise with my time.

- I am an overcomer.

- I shall be prosperous in all my ways.

- My fruit shall come forth in its appropriate season.

APPLICATION

Make the Time for H.E.R.

To everything *there is* a season, A time for every purpose under heaven:
Ecclesiastes 3:1

Here are a few principles, activities, and strategies I learned from the scripture:

1. There's a time and a season for every activity under the sun.

2. Every vision has an appointed time and a specific time frame attached to it.

3. Every goal must be done in its appropriate season.

4. Prioritizing is King.

5. Put a demand on your time.

Prioritizing

Visions, goals, dreams, and desires are manifested when they are nurtured. Therefore, we must cultivate what God has placed on the inside of us. The most effective way to ensure that you are nurturing what God has given is to create a priority list. This list will guide you in your daily, weekly, and monthly activities so that everything can get its proper attention. The key to having an effective priority list is to make it your top priority. If things do not fit within your priority scope, you may not want to invest your time in them. I'm not saying you should not have any playtime. But you cannot be all play and not work. If we work hard, we should play harder. Sometimes, you have to minimize or eliminate unproductive activities until the goal is accomplished to achieve your desires. The modification will be based on the target, your time frame to achieve it, how much attention it's going to need, and how much time you must put into it. Your priority list should drive at least 80% of your time.

Make a list of your top five priorities

1. _____

2. _____

3. _____

4. _____

5. _____

Vision Management Plan

Develop a vision management plan to plan for the success of your vision. This plan will give you a visual representation of the work and effort you will put into what God has placed in your heart. This management plan should include the specific times you work on your goals, daily and weekly action items to complete, resources acquired and needed, and success indicators.

Capture Your Vision

> "Where there is no vision, the people perish: but he that keepeth the law, happy is he" (Proverbs 29:18 KJV).

What is the goal you would like to accomplish? Capture your vision on paper.

Goal: _____

Action Step: These are small steps you will take to complete your goal.

1._____ Complete By: _____

2.._____ Complete By: _____

List potential obstacles. Provide solutions for your obstacles.

Identify Your Resources

List your current resources: List your required resources:

_____   _____

_____   _____

_____   _____

_____   _____

Who do you need on the team and in what capacity?

_____   _____

_____   _____

_____   _____

Progress Indicators:

_____

_____

_____

_____

Plan Your Time

Incorporate your goals into your daily schedule or to-do list. Intentionally plan to work on them for 30 minutes or more a day. You will be amazed at what you produce in 365 days by continuously working on it 30 minutes a day. You must intentionally plan your 24 hours if you desired to live life to the fullest. To assist you with time adjustment, track your current activity and how much time you spend on them for one month. It will give you a snapshot of you currently spend your time. This will help you identify time wasters and distractions. Use a time logger app to track your time or you can write it down manually. Each time you change activities, write down the name of the activity and the time you started it.

Name of the activity: _____   Time:

_____

Name of the activity: _____   Time:

_____

Name of the activity: _____   Time:

_____

Contingency planning sheet.

1. Identify past things that have caused you to sacrifice God's word so you will not repeat it.

    a. Is it fear, unhealthy habits with time, pain, etc.?

2. Develop a list of resources that can help you not return to those habits.

3. How are you going to cut it off?

4. Follow through with the plan.

5. Identify healthy barriers or safeguards to keep you from sacrificing the word of God for your life.

Count the Cost

How much does it cost your family financially, spiritually, emotionally, and physically on a daily basis because you have not moved in your vision?

_____

_____

_____

_____

REFLECTIONS

Take a moment and write down your thoughts

_____

_____

_____

_____

_____

_____

_____

_____

_____

_____

_____

_____

_____

_____

_____

_____

_____

_____

_____

_____

_____

_____

_____

_____

_____

_____

_____

_____

_____

ABOUT THE AUTHOR

Kingdom Strategist, Blueprint Builder, and Spiritual Midwife **Dr. Derashay Zorn** is an international business coach, best-selling author, and expert in the art of **unleashing purpose, developing dreams, and expanding untapped potentials within individuals, corporations, and ministries.** Her passion for information technology has led her to obtain a Master of Science in Information System Management, which equipped her to **analyze, develop, and manage systems to birth or expand individuals and entities into the next dimension of kingdom implementation.**

Derashay equips mankind globally as the Founder of the **Kingdom Influencers Network, In The Church™ TV & Radio Broadcast, Divine Order Restoration Ministries (D.O.R.M) International, Kingdom Strategist Firm, Women of Influence Magazine, (D.O.R.M) Publishing,** and many other entrepreneurship endeavors that equip mankind globally. Through her global brands **Kingdom Strategies University® & Preneurs Academy®,** she teaches others **how to maximize their potential and monetize their gifts and talents** as a critical vehicle for fulfilling their purpose, making a significant impact, and brand influence that can instantly and beautifully change the world. Her books and workbook titled **"Abortions In the Church: Divine Strategies to Spiritual Deliverance,"** 31 Ways of Influence V1, & **Meant for My Good: Being Developed In The Midst of the Disaster** are helping others overcome and give birth to their purpose, visions, and dreams. She is a mother, pastor, entrepreneur, consultant, empowerment speaker, mentor, and friend.

Her philosophy is **"A critical tool for self-development is learning how to cultivate, build, and release others into their destinies."**

CONTACT INFORMATION

Email Address: info@derashayzorn.com

Website: www.derashayzorn.com

SOCIAL MEDIA

Twitter: @kbstrategist

Facebook Page: @kingdomstrategist

Instagram: @kingdomstrategist

STAYING WARM WHEN IT'S COLD OUTSIDE
LaWanna Bradford

She is not afraid of the snow for her household: for
all her household are clothed with scarlet.
Proverbs 31:21

When we think of snow, typically, the first thing we think of after admiring the beauty of newly fallen snow is a warm fire and perhaps a comfortable blanket and a cup of hot cocoa. We want to feel insulated, comforted, and protected from the effects that long exposure to the cold can bring. This passage about the virtuous woman succinctly tells us that she is not afraid of the snow, and she and her household are warm and protected. They are not only protected with proper clothing, and they are clothed in scarlet, which during Biblical times represented wealth, position, and power.

The virtuous woman was one of focused discipline. In earlier passages, we learn that she was an individual who daily did the right things to ensure that in times of winter or storms, she and her household would be protected. When we look closer, we realize that this covering extended beyond her family to all members of her household clothed with scarlet. The color scarlet in garments was not only seen as status but was known to retain heat far better than a lighter colored garment.

As women today, we can learn so much from the virtuous woman who, in previous scriptures, we learned that she had an entrepreneurial mind and was very disciplined in what she did, including the management of her finances and her household. Within Proverbs 31, we see where the virtuous woman considered a field and saw that it was good and made her purchase. With her analytical prowess, she looked at an opportunity and assessed if it was investment-worthy. Once she purchased the land, she planted on it, which today would mean that when we make a purchase, we have an opportunity to see what type of return it can provide to us. She then took the harvest and sold it, making more money from that transaction. This woman was a trailblazer for her time as she and successfully uncovered multiple streams of income. With all that she had, she was so positioned that during a storm, or a crisis, when times where things were not as abundant, she did not worry because her family was insulated and protected.

Why is it that two thousand years later, our modern women often do not have sound financial and physical security financial practices in place? We tend to be more consumed with other matters rather than discussions that can help insulate and protect our homes and families in times of lack, constraint, and storms.

The average woman in the US, when she retires at the age of 65, will have less than $17K in retirement income on which to live. Women live paycheck to paycheck more than men. Women, due to several factors, are not saving as much as men. We may have experienced or know someone where there is a raise or a large infusion of funds that have come in, and rather than pausing and assessing how we might be able to use the money and invest it, or allow it to work for us, we often squander it on a depreciating asset.

"FOR IF I DO THIS OF MY OWN WILL, I HAVE A REWARD, BUT IF NOT OF MY OWN WILL, I AM STILL ENTRUSTED WITH A STEWARDSHIP" — 1 CORINTHIANS 9:17

This is one example. It reveals that the virtuous woman has not only prepared for the winter, but there is far more depth than what may appear on the surface. The scripture speaks to her preparation, her status, her diligence, her dedication, and the daily practice of doing the right thing and not squandering funds mindlessly. This does not mean that you cannot enjoy what you earn because with her scarlet clothing representing the finest quality garments, she took pleasure in enjoying some of what she was earning. However, the scripture begins with addressing her mindset. She was not afraid for her household, which leads us to believe that she ensured they had all they needed to weather through any storm.

Today we have a financial crisis facing women, yet they are unwilling to have those critical conversations and receive the education needed to make the best financial decisions for themselves and their family. This scripture creates assumptions that somehow she received the education and guidance on not only how to manage a household, but to be the fiscal steward of her household, and one who contributed financially in such a meaningful way that it eliminated any worry, stress, and fear she may have had. She knew all was well, and she knew she had done the right things to put life in order for her family. Many of us may have enough reserves for one or two months, but do we have enough to sustain us for the long-term. This is all about a mindset. The word says do not be afraid. We should not worry about tomorrow because tomorrow has enough worries of its own. We are to be focused on this day. The virtuous woman was not afraid. She did not have a mindset of fear, and the scriptures tell us if we are not operating in fear, we are operating from a state of power and a sound mind.

We must ask ourselves what is our mindset, and how do we adjust it and become disciplined in our thoughts and actions so that we do not live a life of fear. Her actions show that with all she does, everything is for her household. There is much we can learn from our daily actions. Are we investing our money on many frivolous things that if there is a major emergency like a car needing repair or a plane ticket is needed to fly to the aid of a family member, we don't have the reserves needed to address the crisis? If we only pause and make the better decision of being a disciplined financial steward, then we would not have all the anxiety, stress, and fear that comes from not having the *just-in-case* preparations in place.

This does not mean if you do all of the things to keep your house in order and protected, challenges will not come. However, we would be better prepared to handle the shifts and changes that life brings. The virtuous woman, when you explore what she was doing from a financial standpoint, was preparing. She was an entrepreneur and an investor. She assessed the profitability of her investment. Then, she determines what else she could do to expand those investments. When we think about our lives and what we are doing as women, we have to realize that sitting on the sidelines and doing nothing is an option. It is a choice that we can take; however, it is an option that will ultimately lead to peril. This is not what we want. Instead, we want to be enriched and empowered through the testament of the virtuous woman.

Many look at the virtuous woman and see this as an unobtainable woman in her countless traits of *perfection*. However, when you dissect the scriptures and allow the Spirit to speak to your heart, you are able to see that what she did is achievable. The high standards of the virtuous woman are based on discipline and decision. She decided and continued in a daily discipline. This yielded fruits of her labor, which provided her with the comfort and security in knowing that she and her household were protected.

We must take the time to discipline ourselves, adjust, and determine what is our mindset. Are we operating with a hope methodology, i.e., I hope everything will be ok? Are we constantly crying out to God, "Help help help," refusing to acknowledge that He has done everything and has given us everything. It is time for us to make a decision and be disciplined. God can give us abundance, but if we do not know how to manage it, it can be fleeting. He can pour blessings upon us, but if we do not know how to manage them when winter comes and we go to our bank accounts or in the pantry, they are empty. What we want to do is consider the lessons behind the virtuous woman and ask are there any gaps or limitations in our thinking. Are we blocking certain blessings because of our mental mindset? Have we decided that today is the day we are going to make a difference and be the best we can and be a good steward over all that we have? Will you be able to sit in a seat of comfort and faith and not worry about tomorrow because you know that all is well because you have done all you can do with all that you have been blessed with?

SUPPLICATION

Lord God, I pray you will help me to be a great steward in my life. Help me to be more fiscally responsible for all that you have given me. Help me to think about what I may be able to do to better insulate my family from the unknowns that can happen in life – from the shifts and changes that may happen. Help me to not only learn from those who are teaching but to be a teacher to my family. Help me believe that my family is clothed in scarlet – all my household is clothed in scarlet, and we are insulated, protected, and shielded from the snow. I thank you that I do not have a spirit of fear, but one of power, love, and a sound mind. In Jesus' name, so let it be said, so let it be done. Amen.

AFFIRMATION

I am the head and not the tail.
I am blessed in the city and the field.
The fruit of my labor is blessed.
I have the spirit of power, love, and a sound mind.
I believe no harm shall come to me or my household.
I am faithful over all that God has given me.
I invest wisely and am a good steward.
I consider the costs of all my investments.
I know that every good and perfect gift is from God.

APPLICATION

Seek Daily to be a Good Financial Steward.

Think about the things you can do to help you better control your finances and prepare for life's rainy days and snowstorms.

Write an *I will daily seek ways to become a good financial steward* statement. In this statement, you will want to identify what things you will do to begin making better financial choices and saving.

I will look for the signs and listen to the sounds of those in need.

Proclamation:

I will work toward understanding the signs I receive and pray against them. (Challenge or Opposition)

_____
_____
_____
_____
_____

To Overcome my challenges, I will (solution).

_____
_____
_____
_____

Overcoming Scripture: Write scriptures from the word of God you can have as a reminder when trusting the signs you receive from seeking your purpose and passion.

_____
_____
_____
_____

Find a person who can be an accountable partner for you to work on and increase your awareness and faith moving towards your passion.

_____
_____
_____
_____

REFLECTIONS

Take a moment and write down your thoughts

_____

_____

_____

_____

_____

_____

_____

_____

_____

_____

_____

_____

_____

_____

_____

_____

_____

_____

_____

_____

_____

_____

_____

_____

_____

_____

ABOUT THE AUTHOR

LaWanna Bradford is a serial entrepreneur and global leader in the strategic planning and performance management arena. She is a thought leader and business management consultant who applies strategic thinking and business management concepts to maximize efficiency and effectiveness and identify both business and life opportunities for improvement and growth. She is the COO of The Bradford Group, a commercial and investment mortgage brokerage, and the principal of The Bradford Group Consulting, a business management consulting firm. As a change agent, she leverages her 30+ years of experience working with federal and private industries and small businesses to guide individuals toward achieving growth, understanding their market position, and increasing awareness of the customers they serve. LaWanna is certified in Strategic Planning and Quality Management and Georgia Oglethorpe Board Examiner's Training. She holds a Bachelor of Arts in Sociology from the University of Arizona and a graduate degree in Administrative Organization and Management from Golden Gate University Graduate School of Public Administration. Her passion for shifting paradigms that allow women to elevate to the highest versions of themselves is magnified in the Celebrate You Women Embracing Wellness movement that she envisioned and co-founded. LaWanna is an international best-selling author, public speaker, trainer, philanthropist, artist, avid reader, and writer who loves nature and spending time with her family. She believes life should be embraced in the moment of now ad positive transformation and lasting impact in life and business is achieved one strategy at a time.

CONTACT INFORMATION

Email Address: lawanna@bradfordgroupmtg.com

Website: https://www.bradfordgroupmtg.com

SOCIAL MEDIA

Twitter: @LaWannaBradford

Facebook Page: @lawanna.bradford.3

Facebook Business: @bradfordgroupmtg

Facebook Business: @bradfordgroupconsulting

LinkedIn: lawannabradford

OUR UNIQUENESS, IS IT CREATING AN IMPACT?
Barbara Beckley

Give her of the fruit of her hands; and let her own
works praise her in the gates.
Proverbs 31:31

Why do we work so hard to fit in when we were born to stand out? We don't need to work so hard to show people who we are, but we must understand our uniqueness. This will show others how amazing and incredible we are regarding our gifts, talents, and values. I looked up the definition of uniqueness to understand how it relates to an individual. I found out that the quality of being the only one of his kind is celebrating each individual's essence. It is the quality of being particularly fantastic, memorable, or unusual. I also had a conversation with a friend of mine a few months ago; I asked the question, "What makes you unique?" and they responded, "It's funny you asked me that question. I had the same question from another friend a few weeks ago." Oh, I was interested when the other individual asked the question to them; my friend mentioned the snowflake story. I was a little bit confused because I wondered what snowflakes had to do with uniqueness, so, I asked my friend to continue. He explained that all snowflakes are unique because each ice crystal has a unique path to go to the ground; they will float through different clouds of different temperatures and different levels of moisture, which means the ice crystal will be unique from any other snowflake.

GOD HAS GIVEN EACH OF YOU A GIFT FROM HIS GREAT VARIETY OF SPIRITUAL GIFTS.

1 PETER 4:10-11

I thought it was so impressive that millions of snowflakes fall to the ground, and each one has a distinct pattern. I looked at that and compared it to humanity. We have a uniqueness, separate from others. We need to hone in on what gives us that one of a kind quality.

I thought the story was fascinating. It explained three points. The first step was to understand our uniqueness, to learn how it can affect others, and how to move forward in our individuality.

Understanding Our Uniqueness

The first part of understanding our true uniqueness is realizing we have gifts, talents, and values. We should also request feedback from our peers about how we come across to make adjustments if needed. We must recognize our real purpose, passion, and drive that moves us daily. Just as every human has a different thumbprint, the gifts and talents inside of us are different from others.

We must also recognize what draws us near and the specific goals we consistently work towards. These are some of the signs of finding out our gifts, talents, values, and understanding how to bring out our uniqueness. This is our foundation.

Another fact of understanding our uniqueness is confidence, even when we make mistakes. These are learning moments in our lives where we grow. Many people doubt themselves when they make mistakes. If things don't go the way we thought they should, we shouldn't beat ourselves up. However, we must consider that we are still growing and learning who we are. It takes patience and an open mind. We must continue building our confidence, even when we have people telling us we are not in the right place or if we keep making mistakes. It is important to move forward no matter what comes our way. Our purpose and uniqueness will draw us closer to our goals and dreams.

Third, we must love ourselves. God placed us on this earth for a purpose. It doesn't matter how we came into this life. We still have the uniqueness he gave us to do something in the world. It is not just for ourselves but for others. When the hurricanes and mountains come around to say we cannot move forward, the love of God will take away the storms. God stated in his word that he loves us so much that he gave his only begotten son. His purpose was to make sure that everyone in this world had a second chance to live on after this life. God truly loves us, and his love is with US every single day. If we don't love ourselves, we're going against what God believes, and that will not get us to the next level in life.

Learning How Our Uniqueness Impacts Others

How our uniqueness impacts others is so important. Our life's message and everything we do should mean something to others. This creates change. A few months ago, I posted one of my stories in a Facebook group I facilitate. I decided I wanted the information to make a connection; I told the story of when I was 17 and my father passed. My dad didn't die from natural causes. Unfortunately, he was murdered. My dad was my rock. He would play dolls with me at the age of seven and watch the Wizard of Oz with me no matter how many times I wanted to see it. He would look at me and say, "Do you want to see it again?" Then, we would watch it over again. He would always give me big hugs and let me know that I was brilliant and a diamond that was shaping.

In 1985, my dad was taken away from me. I lost it; I went into my bedroom and tore up everything. Then, I fell to the ground crying. My mother was very concerned. She called 911 to make sure I was okay; they took me to the hospital and put me under a 48-hour suicide watch. Of course, I wasn't okay because my dad was gone. I just wanted to end it all. At the same time that the thought crossed my mind, a nurse walked into my room, took my vitals, and turned to walk away, but she looked back and said, "I don't think your dad would want you to take your own life. He loved you too much. He looked at you as a diamond in the rough.

> "OUR UNIQUENESS WILL OPEN UP DOORS FOR OUR GIFTS AND TALENTS TO PROSPER"
>
> - BARBARA BECKLEY

I knew that was a sign. I needed to move forward to make sure no other person, especially women, felt discouraged or not valued. So I told this story on Facebook. The group members shared it out to their page, and then their friends shared it out. I don't even know where the shares were going, which didn't matter. I only wanted to make sure I could make an impact. That same day, I received an email from an individual. They thanked me for posting my story. At the same time this person received the post on Facebook, they were about to give up on their own life. These were their words, "I decided it wasn't going to happen that day because of what you chose to do in your life when you were 17 years old after losing your dad." This is an example of how your story's uniqueness can make a difference in someone else's life that might save them. I am so grateful that I listened to the voice that told me to post that story. It's essential to make our overcoming experiences our message.

Steps to continue to use our uniqueness as an anchor in our life

It's essential to have some steps to go by to move in our uniqueness. First, we must practice listening to our heart, that inner voice. That passion and purpose within will lead and guide us. Most of the time, God is speaking. Secondly, we should never make everything about building relationships with others nor allowing them to be the center of our conversations. We can listen to what they're saying, engage with them, and assist in the areas we can, but our focus must be on what God has called us to do.

Our uniqueness will open up doors for our gifts and talents to prosper in other's lives. We must develop and never be reluctant to learn something new. In every challenge, we will continue to learn.

Overall, we must stand out like the snowflake. We will go through the hurricanes and floods of life, but we must remember those things build our uniqueness. They are the stepping stones of strength so that we can be available for the master's use.

SUPPLICATION

Thank you, Father God, for making me understand the gifts, the talents, and the values you have placed in me to serve you. Thank you for the knowledge through my circumstances and mistakes. We understand not to beat ourselves up but to grow and move forward in our goals. Lord, I thank you for making sure I understand that my life impacts others. You have called me to make connections. You may also work through me to save someone's life. Thank you for helping me to understand myself, to walk in confidence, and love myself. I am thankful for the many talents and gifts you have given me to do your will in this world.

AFFIRMATION

I have gifts and talents from God.

I love myself.

I am confident.

I am bold in God.

I receive any lessons you have called me to learn.

I do not let the storms overtake me.

I am God's child and royalty.

APPLICATION

OUR UNIQUENESS, IS IT CREATING AN IMPACT?

We have to ask ourselves, "What will my gifts and talents do to create an impact that will change lives and situations?" It doesn't always have to be a significant change. It can be a small step, like helping someone in need. We have to build on what we have to help others, and we must take the steps to really be confident in who we are to create the changes needed in the world. When we stand true to our purpose in life, we can make a difference, and others will learn from our example. The following are a few steps on how to understand who we are and how to move forward in helping others in need:

List your gifts and talents. Do not measure them because every gift you have can make a great difference in an individual's life.

_____
_____
_____
_____
_____
_____
_____

Write down your challenges and a few experiences where you were able to move forward and learn from the steps provided in this chapter. This will help when you are talking to others that need to hear hope.

_____
_____
_____
_____
_____
_____
_____

Love Scriptures: Write down a few scriptures from the Word of God that reference the love God has for you.

_____
_____
_____
_____
_____
_____
_____

Ask a close friend or family how you come across in their eyes? This is to get a perspective on how you are around others. (Remember, make sure you are getting your feedback from those who have your best interest at heart.

_____

_____

_____

_____

_____

_____

_____

Look up as many quotes about being an impact and knowing you are special in God's eyes. Be sure to keep them near as a reminder of why it's essential to have that foundation built.

_____

_____

_____

_____

_____

_____

_____

ABOUT THE AUTHOR

Barbara Beckley is a professional keynote speaker, three-time Amazon best-selling author, a purpose strategist, and a social media personality. She is the founder and CEO of the Diamond Factor LLC, which empowers people to understand their PPD (Purpose, Passion, and Drive), especially women, to help them overcome their challenges so they can shine like a diamond in their business and personal lives. For the past nine years, with her communication and leadership skills, Barbara worked her way up to becoming a program quality director, one who provides educational opportunities for over 5500 potential clients. In addition, she has over 30+ years of experience working within the commercial insurance industry as a broker and mentor. In this capacity, Barbara offers webinar trainings, one on one coaching, and keynote presentations concerning personal development. Also, to help increase visibility, she does interviews to promote businesses and/or special causes that include image and content coaching. You can find Barbara on social media, where she loves connecting and sharing tips and strategies on all things concerning your purpose and growth.

CONTACT INFORMATION

Email Address: diamondfactorexperience@gmail.com

SOCIAL MEDIA

Facebook: https://www.facebook.com/groups/DiamondFactorBB/

CHASING GOD IN ME!
Chanda Johnson

"She is clothed with strength and dignity, and she laughs without fear of the future, when she speaks, her words are wise, and she gives instructions with kindness" (Proverbs 31:25-26 NLT).

As you live your life day by day, is there something that you feel on the inside of you that makes you unique? Do you desire greatness from it? Is there something you do not understand, but feel there is more for you to do? Is there something that you feel that is tugging on you on the inside? What you are seeing and feeling is purpose. Breathing every minute gives us the opportunity to allow something to come forth. How can we bring it to the point where it is flourishing, you ask? Seeking God and his guidance is the way to start the birthing of your purpose. In John 14:6, Jesus speaks about being the way, the truth, and the life; therefore, when we want to know which path we need to take to find our purpose, we call on him, praying with thanksgiving petitions and taking the time to listen to his response   He provides us with truth without opinions and assumptions and no secondhand information, and then he allows us to have a life worth living, reaching the destiny that we have been created for. When we seek our purpose, we are chasing God's will in us.

The purpose for our lives, as God has revealed to me, can be compared to a light on the inside of us. Sometimes, it may seem dim or far away from us, but the key is to recognize it and engage with it, so it may become brighter every day as we breathe the breath of life. For example, many years ago, I attended and visited different church services for praise and worship and a sermon I could enjoy. During this time, I heard several sermons over the years but never felt the need to apply it to my life except for a few messages that I received food to chew on. At the time, I heard more whooping and hollering than anything. Therefore, I did not understand anything else they said, so I read the Bible myself to try to gain understanding. Unfortunately, many times I could not remember the message. Now, as I have received different revelations from God, he has me looking back over my life at different situations and experiences I have had. While doing this, I have realized that I have value, and I know there is value in you, too, my sisters and brothers, because the word of God tells us so. Believe me, I had to learn that I needed to chase God in me for myself. I now run after God in me because I know nobody else can, and I am excited about what he has for me to do. Just like the lady with the issue of blood, I had to learn to press my way through the crowd and the chaos, no matter what obstacles or situations I was dealing with. I had to realize that God was, and still is, giving me peace to continue to follow his path and guidance. God has shown me with my past that even as a young child growing up in Atlanta, he was preparing me for greater. While living there, there was a neighbor that did some ungodly things— but the other neighbor taught me prayers and encouraged me to read the Bible. I did not understand until later that that part of the light in me is that I am an intercessor; he also reminded me that sometimes, when I would ride the school bus, I would pray; at that time, I was not aware of the intercession part of myself.

"THERE IS SOMETHING SHINING IN YOU"

— CHANDA JOHNSON

As we look at the virtuous woman in the Bible fearing the Lord, it shows how she reverenced him. In the New Testament, it speaks about praying without ceasing. So, we must reverence him and consistently communicate with him to help prepare us for what is to come; the virtuous woman tried to stay prepared. So I ask you, what are you looking to do about figuring out your purpose? Just to let you know, finding your purpose is not a one day experience; it is a lifelong adventure featuring what the true and living God has placed in you.

Look, there is something shining in you—can you see it or feel it? There is no doubt in my mind that it is there, but you have to see or feel it for yourself. Unfortunately, nobody else can activate it but you. For example, in Proverbs 31:15, it speaks about how the virtuous woman stays up late to make sure necessary task are taken care of and it does not speak of anyone else doing the work for her. She is making sure that everything is done for herself, her family, and ministry. I also had to learn to prioritize my day with God, family, and ministry in that order, sometimes staying up late and getting up early to open myself up to be aligned with God's will. I am still working to better myself and become more consistent at writing down a schedule, so if something happens out of my control and I am unable to finish what was on the agenda, then I just rearrange it in the order as it needs to be done for the next day; in this way, I do not lose focus of what God has placed inside of me. We all need to keep the light burning in us.

Let us just look at this light; it is because of God that it burns on the inside of us. He is the one who has created and implanted in us everything we need to reach our purpose; that is why we must consistently seek God daily for the burning on the inside of us that we often do not understand. We must remember that God has the perfect plan for our good, shown in Jeremiah 29:11; so even though we may not fully know what we are stepping into at that time, we can trust the process because it shows us that it will be for our good. This is when we step out on faith and allow God to order our steps. As long as we are trying to live holy and consistently focusing on the righteous way of living, we can make it to our ultimate purpose. Proverbs 31:20 states that the virtuous woman reached out to the poor and needy. For years, I did not recognize reaching out to the poor and needy as a part of my purpose. In walking in this life, I have also learned that poor and needy does not only refer to low finances, but there are people that are poor in spirit and others that need encouragement and empowerment to continue to seek the light of God in their lives. There is a light inside of us that is connected to every breath we breathe, which helps us acknowledge and remember that we have a purpose, and we must focus on God to arrive at the appointed destination.

When we take our focus off God, we take a chance of losing access to his plan, his power, and his purpose for our lives. In order to keep from missing out on the best life ever, we must submit ourselves, consisting of our whole body, so that we can be a tool that he can use for his glory. Surrendering our lives over to God can seem really hard to do, but once you see the manifestation of his spirit in your life, it leads you to prefer his desires more than your own. God is the only one who has, can, and will bless you beyond your wildest dreams. He has equipped you to help build the kingdom in ways you will not believe until you fully surrender, and then God will allow it to manifest in the right season when it is needed. As you continue to open yourself up to God, he will reveal some of your destiny to you as you are ready to receive it. Make no mistake, when you present yourself back to God, it will sometimes seem that everything in the world is coming against you, so this is where you have to pray and remind yourself that Jesus Christ has made us victorious in our lives because he gave himself for us. So, after you have given your whole being back to God, and at any moment you find yourself in an unwelcoming place, immediately go to find the place where you last felt God's presence—or create a place, because this is how you obtain your peace. You will recognize that this is all a part of His plan

> **"JESUS CHRIST HAS MADE US VICTORIOUS"**
>
> – CHANDA JOHNSON

to mold and shape you into the exact tool He will use to glorify the Lord.

Many times in the molding and shaping, there is pain. Sometimes, it seems unbearable, but because you have already submitted your life back to God, you can be reassured that you are protected and provided strength in the midst of what looks like an unusual storm in your life. At this point, you want to ask God to guide your steps so that you will have nothing to fear about the future. You can also obtain wisdom so that when you speak, you can use it to help guide others to Christ with love. We have to realize that it is all a learning process; it may seem negative, sometimes, but this is where you have to recognize that it is teaching you, what and know that you are built with boldness to press through. Often, we are so frustrated, aggravated, depressed, etc., that we focus on the negative and lose track of all the positive things. Then we end up having to go back through the same test to try to pass it again. Even with the pain, we have to focus on God because he has clothed us with all the strength we need to press through. What we have to realize is that even in the pain, we can take a moment and breathe in and exhale and then say to ourselves, "I am breathing, therefore I know I still have purpose." Many times, this can actually be a part of where the birthing of your destiny is stirred from. This is the part of seeking your purpose where you have to truly trust the process and put in work along with your faith. No matter what, the process is designed to lead you to your purpose because you are specifically made for this journey.

When we recognize our uniqueness and understand there is no one to compare us to, we can see more clearly because we are not comparing our life to others. Each one of us has been made for a special purpose; therefore, the way we grow will be different and the way we are tested will be different; many times, we look at other people's lives and wonder why they are living the way they are living; we may even feel sometimes that others have better possessions than we do. The problem here is we are looking at the current physical situation and not seeking spiritual realm activities because one person can be up today and down tomorrow. So, we cannot look at what others have, but we have to live the life that we have and go to God with great expectations because when you submit to his will, you show God you love him and appreciate him, and he will pour so many blessings out for you that you will not have enough room to receive them.

Remember, there is a light within you that sometimes seems further away than it truly is, but this light is accessible through Jesus Christ by accepting him as your Lord and Savior. As you are surrendering your life to him, all of your boldness and uniqueness will be discovered; the closer you get to your ultimate purpose, the brighter his light in you will shine which will extend to where others can see the glow that beams outwardly and will show the true love of God in your life, even with any bad choices that we have made.

Yes, God can turn negative thoughts you have about yourself and make it into a masterpiece. I saw in the first marriage I was in; within the first three months of my first marriage, I felt that I made a mistake. But because I did not want my child to grow up without his biological father, I stayed, trying to make it work. I dealt with domestic violence, both emotional and physical, in this relationship. I battled with divorce in my mind for years because I believed that if I divorced, I would be going against the vows I made. A few years into the marriage, I dreamed that there were inappropriate actions taking place in the marriage. Then one day, while in church singing praises unto God, he released me from that situation and told me it was time for me to let it go. I doubted what I heard at first, but there was a boldness that came forth. I did it, and I had no worries about how bills were going to get paid or anything. Otherwise, that may have been difficult for me, but God gave me an unexplainable peace. That is how I know it was God. Then I had several people telling me there was a glow on me they had not seen before. At that time, I did not realize what it was until God reminded me of this experience when I was seeking him on what I needed to do about the women's ministry and the assignment on my life. He immediately showed me that he is the light that allows his people to glow. The light is God working in you; he is the one who brings the glow upon you that many people do not understand.

"GOD CAN TURN NEGATIVE THOUGHTS YOU HAVE ABOUT YOURSELF AND MAKE IT INTO A MASTERPIECE"

– CHANDA JOHNSON

Now, I know that we cannot stop seeking God for our purpose because sometimes, we are only serving in just some of the gifts that we have been equipped with. There has to be consistency in pursuing what God has created us to be. Helping some of the people in my life has only been part of what God is doing in me. God matures us through tests to equip us for each level of our journey; there has to be some suffering and pressing to help us be prepared for each elevation. Using myself as an example, God has directed me to go forth with a women's ministry that I had sat on for two years during this pandemic in May 2020. In 2018, he had given me the name G.L.O.W which stands for God's Love On Women. I felt I did not know where to go from there. As I continued to pursue, pray, and read the word, to me, it seemed like I was not getting anything. But now, I look back and I remember that I kept having an eagerness to read the parables, but I kept procrastinating. Finally, I was not able to work due to internet issues, so I went to the Bible. The title for the first women's conference came from the parable of the ten virgins. God gave me the title "Keep Your Light Burning", and the subtitle "Are You in Position?" These titles spoke to me first. This is when I truly started to submit myself totally to God by listening to what he was speaking to me through thoughts and feelings, and seeing in visions and dreams.

I must advise you, as you submit daily to God's will, the enemy will try to attack, but you have to resist so he will flee. Stay the course; if you fall, get back up! You have to live this journey we call life, so why not live it to the best that you can be and glow for God? When you are clothed with the strength that God provides to you, then even the enemies have to respect you! We stand in victory because of Jesus being the sacrifice; so no matter what any evil spirit tries to throw at us, we always win because of the love our Father consistently pours out on us. Therefore, you do not have to worry about issues you may have or the surrounding chaos. Our Lord provides strength and an unconditional love that allows our light to become brighter and brighter as we consistently focus on him for our purpose. It's time for us to G.L.O.W for God; purpose is revealed through the pressure. So now, can you see that beautiful light within you? If not yet, then let me help you; start to pursue it now because God Loves On Women, too!

SUPPLICATION

Father, I want to thank you for even taking the time to create me. If it were not for you, I would not be here right now. This is one way I know that you love me and that I am special to you. Lord, it states in your word that everything you created is good. So, I come to you today in humbleness, wanting to seek your will for my life; I want to seek your face, asking that you forgive me of all my sins, knowingly and unknowingly. I believe that Jesus lived and died and rose from the grave for us. Thank you for our Comforter, who helps guide me in what you have created me to do. Lord, I am asking that you would put me on the potter's wheel and make me over again, that I may receive your revelations more clearly. Father, I ask that you renew my mind and clear my ear and eye gates that I may discern your voice better. Also, I ask that you restore me to the original state you created me in and release in me consistent knowledge and wisdom that I need to help activate my gifts, talents, and purpose that it may be used for your glory!

Father, it states in your word, whatever I bind on earth, you will bind in heaven, and what I release on earth, you will release in heaven. So, right now, in the name of Jesus, I bind up any negativity, hindrances, and obstacles that will try to come against me as I walk with you into my purpose. I bind any type of fear, strongholds, backlashes, curses, demons, witches, warlocks, and anything that is negative and not of you, God. Now, I release peace, joy, love, hope, strength, wisdom, knowledge, and I release a pressing in my life of everything you have placed in me, that it be birthed in its season for your glory, in Jesus' name. Thank you, Lord, for allowing your word to be a lamp on my feet and a light on my path; continue to guide me each and every day in Jesus' name. Amen!

AFFIRMATION

I help guide my family and ministry with love.
I am living for a great purpose.

I am loved by my heavenly Father.

I move as the light leads me to move.

I am beautiful inside and out.

I will let no worldly thing separate me from my purpose.

I consistently seek God for his will in my life.

I do not compare myself to others because I am uniquely made.

I have a new mind and a cleaned heart because God is aligning me.

I speak life into myself and the people around me.

I know that the Holy Spirit guides me daily for my purpose.

I know God has the best plan and purpose for my life.

I am nothing without God; that is why I trust his plan and will not quit seeking him for my purpose.

I know that the Holy Spirit dwells in me.

I know God's plan, his power, and purpose go hand in hand.

I hear clearly from God.

I am determined to complete my ultimate purpose.

I have the light of God in me.

I have the strength of God when I feel weak.

I speak with boldness and wisdom.

I love chasing God in me.

APPLICATION

Journal daily

(Write what stands out to you in your thoughts and feelings and everything you remember about your visions and dreams.)

Pursue and **P**ray to God

- Talk to God and listen to him daily.
- Look for God in your life and engage with him.
- Create a place for just you and God to communicate.

Untouched by the Ways of the World

- Resist the devil, and he will flee.
- Remember the promises God has told you.
- Let no negativity cause you to doubt.

Read the Word of God (Bible)

- Many times, God will reveal things to you while reading his word.
- Often, you can read the chapter or verses and obtain a new revelation as you build a better relationship with the Lord.

Pray Even More

- Communicate with God in a way that is comfortable for you.
- Be consistent in talking to him.
- Take the time to listen to what he is saying.

Open All Your Senses to Hear God Speak

- God can use your eyes, mind, ears, smell, and touch to speak to you.
- Protect what he gives you until he tells you it is time to release it.

Submit Daily to God's Will

- Present everything back to God, including your whole body.
- Allow the Holy Spirit to guide you.
- Allow God to show you and be willing to adjust to the change.

Expect Greatness

- Remember his promises in his word and what he has spoken to you.
- Speak life into yourself, even where you think it does not matter.
- Always know God wants the best for you.

REFLECTIONS

Take a moment and write down your thoughts

_____

_____

_____

_____

_____

_____

_____

_____

_____

_____

_____

_____

_____

_____

_____

_____

_____

_____

_____

_____

_____

_____

_____

_____

_____

_____

_____

_____

ABOUT THE AUTHOR

Elder Chanda Johnson is a worshiper of God who enjoys helping others, many times putting herself last. She helps others; however, God leads her while she assists her husband, Bishop-Elect Antonio Johnson, with the vision God has placed in him at God's Church Ministries, where we currently worship in Forest Park, Georgia.

She is also a lifelong learner who appreciates teaching and learning new things and ways to be creative. Elder Johnson has obtained her Master's Degree in Education from Ashford University in 2014, and now, she desires to use this knowledge and passion for God's glory.

As she continues to seek God for constant guidance for her purpose in life, God gave her instructions in 2018 for a women's ministry with the name G.L.O.W, which stands for God's Love on Women, where women come together in unity to encourage each other and take that to encourage every man, woman, and child that God leads them to. He allowed her to go forth with the first annual conference in May 2020 titled, "KEEP YOUR LIGHT BURNING," using Matthew 25:1-13 to inspire others to continue to stand on the word and consistently seek their purpose from our Almighty God!

CONTACT INFORMATION

Email Address: minister.cjohnson.2018@gmail.com

Website:

SOCIAL MEDIA

Twitter:

Facebook Page: Chanda Johnson

Instagram: @chanda_johnson7

PERCEPTION IS KEY
Reverend Rita M. Henderson

"She sees that her trading is profitable, and her lamp
does not go out at night"
Proverbs 31:18, NIV

Perception is something we all have inside of us. Often, many of our actions are determined by how we perceive things to be. And how we perceive things is based on what we hear or see. Yet, our perception of words, people, and events can be entirely wrong. Why? This brings us to the definition of "perception."

Perception is defined as using the senses or the mind to acquire information about the environment or a particular situation. As we have a natural perception, we also have spiritual perception. Spiritual perception is impossible to grasp for carnality. We must understand that anytime our senses or mind are involved, there is potential for error. Thus, until our mind is completely renewed spiritually, our perception has the potential for distortion.

"And do not be conformed to this world, but be transformed by the renewing of your mind, that you may prove what is that good and acceptable and perfect will of God" (Romans 12:2, NKJV).

We can only renew our minds through the word of God. When we constantly incline our minds to God's word, we can perceive things correctly through the help of the Holy Spirit. In Proverbs 31:18, the woman perceived her trading was profitable. Prior to this, the woman was spiritually perceptive to know the original blueprint for her life – trading. Her perception helped her to discover her purpose, and this gave her confidence in her abilities. Therefore, she found great comfort and good success in her labors. Woman of God! Perception is the key to discovering your purpose. You can't achieve true greatness and fulfillment if you don't know why God created you.

There's no creation of God that doesn't have a purpose. Birds were created to fly, the sun is created to provide light during the day, and trees are made to produce fruits. God has also created every human for a purpose. Until you know what God is demanding from you, there's no way you can actually exploit the innate abilities He has deposited in you. That is why perception is so important in our lives. Perception enables us to see and hear what God is saying about us. The question is, "Do you see things the way God sees them?"

What are you seeing?

"For all the land that you see, I will give to you and your offspring forever" (Genesis 13:15, NIV).

What you see is very important. Not only that, how you see what you see is also crucial. You are not bigger than your vision. What you see today may be the limit of where you can go. God wants the best for you in life. He wants you to be successful, productive, and excellent in everything you do. Therefore, He requires that you see correctly.

"IT IS NOT EASY, BUT IT IS NECESSARY!"

In Jeremiah 1:11-12, Jeremiah says, "The word of the Lord came to me: What do you see, Jeremiah? I see the branch of an almond tree," I replied. The Lord said to me, you have seen correctly, for I am watching to see that my word is fulfilled."

When you see what God is seeing, you will be confident to channel your abilities into what He wants you to do. For example, let's say you're naturally good at cooking, and God wants you to set up a restaurant. This is where spiritual perception comes in. If you can't perceive what He is asking you to do, you won't be able to reach the level of prosperity He wants for you.

"For God may speak in one way, or in another, yet man does not perceive it" (Job 33: 14, NKJV).

Where are you spiritually, on a mountain top or in the valley? For instance, someone who climbs a mountain top will have a broader view of the environment than the person in the valley. Your spiritual height will determine how wide you will see and hear (perceive) what God is saying concerning you. Woman of God, you can attain spiritual growth when you give yourself to the constant study of God's word and prayer. Then, you will have full access to God's purpose for your life.

Sometimes, we may face challenges that blind us from comprehending God and His voice. In these circumstances, we must guard against those things getting in the way of perceiving when God is near. We must let our focus be on God and not on the challenges.

Fuel your Purpose with your Passion

"…and her lamp does not go out at night" (Proverbs 31:18, NIV).

Dr. Myles Munroe said, "Purpose is the master of motivation and the mother of commitment." Once you've discovered God's purpose for your life, you must fuel and follow it with an unyielding passion so that you can achieve maximum productivity and prosperity. Listen to this: You can never achieve meaningful success in anything you are not passionate about.

The woman in Proverbs 31:18 is personally driven. She knows there is profit in all labor; thus, she does not waste time talking unnecessarily. Once she settles on a plan, she puts in extra effort to make it pan out. She's diligent in her duties and makes sure she completes her tasks. The Proverbs 31:18 woman succeeds in everything she does because she perseveres energetically and does not quit until the goal is obtained. Aim to become this kind of woman!

Woman of God, it's time to rise. It's time to expand your thinking and dominate your world. You must excuse yourself from the thought that man has to be the breadwinner or the productive one. You can match or even exceed him in your areas of expertise and responsibility.

Like the Proverbs 31 woman, keep your lamp burning! Work while others are sleeping, and don't give up on your dreams. You can dominate in that particular field God has called you to function, including business, politics, health, education, music, information technology, and so on. Continue to follow your purpose with passion.

"PURPOSE PLUS PASSION EQUALS PROSPERITY,"

Hold fast to God's Word

God told Joshua in Joshua 1:8, saying, "Keep this Book of the Law always on your lips; meditate on it day and night, so that you may be careful to do everything written in it. Then, you will be prosperous and successful."

When you constantly read, study, and meditate on the word of God, spiritual wisdom is imparted into your life. For example, if you are not ready to meditate on the promises of God for your life into financial prosperity, you'll never have the financial wisdom to prosper in finances.

The financial wisdom God gives to each individual may differ from one

that He will give to others. That's why you shouldn't copy other people's blueprint from God. Woman of God, go to God directly and receive your own from Him. He has different pathways to success and prosperity for everyone. He wants to help you and liberate you from financial bondage. Are you listening to Him?

"THIS FAITH WORKS!"

Many face financial difficulties today because they're not creating time to meditate on God's promises to them financially. They are too busy trying to copy other people's wisdom instead of listening to God's voice to lead and guide them out of their financial difficulties.

You must learn to wait on the Lord, and this habit has to be cultivated by faith. If you want to perceive spiritual truth, you must wait on the Lord as you meditate on His promises both day and night. It is not difficult at all if you can only put your heart into it. When you put God's word in your heart, it produces the spiritual result that your inner spirit has always desired. The word of God is not only food to the heart, mind, and body; it is also the pathway that leads to success and prosperity.

Finally, as you make sacrifices to spend time with God, through meditation and praying in the spirit regularly, your spiritual perception is sharpened, and God will also spend time with you. You will be successful and prosperous in everything that you purpose to do in life.

SUPPLICATION

Dear Father, help me to sharpen my spiritual perception so I can discover your purpose and plans for my life. I need spiritual wisdom to fulfill my destiny and purpose, and I know I can only get it through your word, so Lord, I pray that you give me the desire and love for your word every day and night. I ask that you pour out your blessings upon my life, business, career, and family. Lord, your word tells me in Genesis 26:12, "Then, Isaac sowed in that land and reaped in the same year a hundredfold, and the Lord blessed him." As you helped Isaac to flourish in the land, help me to be fruitful and reap a hundredfold in everything I do.

Oh God, let none of my labor or efforts be wasted, show me where to go, what to do, and where to invest to make massive profits. You are the all-knowing and all-sufficient God; I ask that you reveal business ideas that work. I will be patient and continue to wait for your divine direction and instruction. Lord, your word says in Isaiah 40:31, "But those who wait on the Lord Shall renew their strength…" Please renew my strength and equip me with everything I need to succeed in my career and business. Like the woman in Proverbs 31:18, help me to keep my lamp always burning. Endow me with the required mental skill to execute my job correctly and handle them to make maximum profits.

I come against every form of failure and bankruptcy in my finances. I claim divine favor, divine wisdom, abundant prosperity, increased sales, new product ideas, divine helpers, and the release of finances. Your word tells me in Malachi 3:11, "And I will rebuke the devourer for your sakes…" Lord, I pray that you rebuke every devourer over my life, finances, business, and family. I put my confidence in you as my sustainer, and I secure my blessings in your powerful name.

Lord Jesus, help me to be diligent in all my dealings. Take me to the next level, allow me to stand before great people of influence, and move my generation. Heavenly Father, I don't just want to be wealthy and successful in life. I want to fulfill the purpose you have for me and help me fulfill divine destiny in Jesus' name. Amen.

AFFIRMATION

I am here on purpose, for a purpose.

My knowledge is valuable, and I deserve to be well compensated.

My talents and skills are needed; what I create brings value to the marketplace.

 I will not allow satan to still my joy – done is always better than perfect.

I can do all things through Christ who strengthens me.

APPLICATION

My Passion is: _____

_____

_____

My Purpose is: _____

_____

_____

God has equipped me to serve in the following capacity:

    1. _____

    2. _____

    3. _____

My experiences have made me an expert in:_____

_____

_____

I am saying "No More" to: _____

Within One Month, I will: _____

Within Six Months, I will: _____

Within One Year, I will: _____

REFLECTIONS

Take a moment and write down your thoughts

_____

_____

_____

_____

_____

_____

_____

_____

_____

_____

_____

_____

_____

_____

_____

_____

_____

_____

_____

_____

_____

_____

_____

_____

_____

_____

ABOUT THE AUTHOR

I am a 2x Amazon best-selling author, speaker, and self-publishing coach who helps Five-Fold Ministers plant the seeds of confidence, harvest their self-faith, and clarify their life's vision so that they can birth faith-based businesses that serve, scale, and succeed.

Also known as The Spiritual Midwife, I have taught hundreds of ministers how to birth their purpose and monetize their God ordained talents and acquired skill set by building successful faith-based businesses.

From coaching women on how to launch membership communities to providing hopeful entrepreneurs with the foundational tools to build profitable businesses, I continue to answer the call to assist fellow ministers in pursuing profit-generating, purpose-driven paths.

My own blossoming stemmed from a divine moment in 2011 that drove me away from the roads of hardship – $100K in debt, a foreclosed home, and car repossession despite my having a good yet unfulfilling government job – and steered me straight into my own profitable faith-based business that allows me to live the emotionally, spiritually, and financially free life that I have always dreamed of.

CONTACT INFORMATION

Email Address: reverendrita@5foldpublishing.com

Website: www. 5foldpublishing.com

SOCIAL MEDIA

Twitter:

Facebook Page: facebook.com/prophetesrita.Henderson/

Instagram: reverend_rita

THE WIFE OF NOBLE CHARACTER
Temecka Smith

---

*"Who can find a virtuous woman? for her price is far
above rubies"
(Proverbs 31:10).*

Women come in many variations and we all come from different backgrounds. There always seems to be one common interest that we have had since childhood. The dream of one day meeting Mr. Right and having the elaborate wedding we all admittedly or not have always envisioned. As we grow up, we are persuaded by culture with Disney princess movies and fairy tales that paint the picture of the joy that is felt when the right one comes along. Have you ever noticed how the movie stops playing on the wedding day? The culture makes it appear like the only preparation you need for marriage is to make sure your beauty and body mirrors the actress of the year. However, I believe we have done women and young girls everywhere such an injustice. We have not prepared them for reality but rather for a fairy-tale.

As many of you know, marriage is far from what we have been presented. I want to take the liberty to tell the truth and speak the wisdom that true women of God passed down to me pertaining to marriage. Let me stop there. I said, "True women of God" passed down wisdom and truth to me. My heart goes out to young women in this generation. In these days, true women of God are not teaching younger women as the scripture says in Titus 2:4 because they are too busy trying to stay young forever. But I thank God for the few real ones that the Lord placed around me. I don't believe I would be in a nineteen-year marriage had it not been for their wisdom.

Pouring into those looking to be married is a passion of mine. Marriages are a sweet spot the Lord has anointed me for because of the refining fire He has taken my marriage through. My goal is to be used as a voice of truth to that young woman in waiting or to the woman about to walk away from her marriage because she feels it has run its course. Marriage comes with many trials but also many joys. Many are leaving their marriage because no one told them it is hard work. They were only told that the preparation stops at the ring, the dress, and the reception, but it is far more than that. Thank you for trusting me to pour what I know from my cup into yours. I am not coming from a place of perfection but from experience.

Being married for nineteen years has come with many ups and downs, but it is one of the biggest blessings the Lord has ever given me. It has made me become the best version of myself, getting here did not come easy. My marriage prospering took me being willing to sacrifice and laying down my life daily. Sacrifice is a word that very rarely comes up in these times. Marriage could even be defined by the word sacrifice. A lot of women are ready to put on the dress, but they are not willing to put the needs of their spouse before their own. Sacrifice is the beginning of being a wife of noble character. I know you are thinking—what about the men? I completely agree that the flourishing of a marriage doesn't just weigh on the wife. However, this chapter is about being a wife of noble character. Men still need to do their part, but 'virtuous woman' this is for you.

I chose the title "The Wife of Noble Character" because that defines the woman described in the book of Proverbs. Her character was impeccable. Character is the moral qualities distinctive to an individual. Character is who you are as a person not based on your looks. The women who groomed me into the wife I am today put an emphasis on being well-rounded. Ladies, being a wife is so much deeper than just being beautiful.

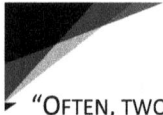

> "OFTEN, TWO BROKEN PEOPLE WILL COME TOGETHER AND BECAUSE THEY EACH HAVE NOT OVERCOME THEIR INDIVIDUAL BROKENNESS THEIR MARRIAGE STRUGGLES"

There is nothing wrong with being beautiful, but have substance, as my mother would tell me. Bring something to the table when you come into union with your man. I have counseled so many women who had requirements for their future spouses that they themselves could not meet. If you look at the qualities of the Virtuous woman, she was not just beautiful but a major asset to that man. She made beautiful fabrics for her husband, and the Book of Proverbs even says that she provided food for her household. In today's term, the virtuous woman was not *lazy* she was a hard worker, and she was not her husband's trophy but his helpmate. These qualities were instilled in me growing up. I promise you that marriage is work, but it is a lot easier when both you and your spouse pull your weight. I have found that you attract people who are like minded to you. If you were to meet my husband, you would find that we have very similar qualities. That is the way marriage should be. You are complimenting your spouse—not making your spouse complete.

Often, two broken people will come together and because they each have not overcome their individual brokenness their marriage struggles. Believe me, virtuous woman, looking for a man to complete you will only lead to more brokenness. As I said earlier, my own marriage has not been a cakewalk. We have not always been at the place we are now. There were many stormy seasons when I thought that walking away was the best decision, but let me tell you, I am so thankful I held on to my marriage. If I had left, I would not be enjoying the many blessings I am now. One thing I want to point out is that the only way for a marriage to work is for it to be centered around Christ. I really cannot express that enough.

The beautiful truth about life is at any moment, you can start over. If you have been reading this, and maybe you feel you have fallen short in some areas, or maybe you weren't equipped with this wisdom when you said, "I do," I want to encourage you to start today. Start being the woman of God you have been called to be as soon as you finish this chapter. In Deuteronomy, the Bible tells us that we have the choice to choose life or death. You have every ability to become the virtuous woman or a wife with noble character because Christ is in you. To the wife in a struggling marriage, I empower you to choose to be the virtuous woman. Choose to be her despite who your husband chooses to be, and trust the Lord to move in your marriage. While you are letting the Lord work on the inside of you, pray and ask the Lord to work on your husband. As I said, marriage takes work, and it is a process. Believe me, if you make Christ the center of your life and marriage, the Lord will do the rest.

> "VIRTUOUS WOMAN, YOU ARE THE GOOD THING."

Maybe you are reading this, and you are waiting on the Lord to bring you the one you were made to walk this earth with. I want to empower you to prepare yourself while you wait. Preparing means letting the Lord heal you and becoming whole. Find out who you are. I often tell those I counsel "date yourself." Knowing who you are and becoming whole is so powerful because it is easy to let pain choose our spouse. Becoming a wife of noble character is a process but every day you get to choose. Many of these precious nuggets of wisdom were passed down to me, and I pray that they are a blessing to you on either your journey of singleness or in the midst of your marriage. Remember that you have value. In fact, the scriptures say, "when a man finds a wife, he finds a good thing." Virtuous woman, you are the good thing. Heal from your pain and center your life around Christ. Choosing to do those two things were the best decision I ever made. Virtuous woman, don't allow anyone to tell you that marriage is just about the ring, the dress, and the reception. Believe me, marriage is hard work, but it is one of the most beautiful things the Lord has given us.

We have talked a lot about the preparation before the wedding, but I would like to take a moment and tackle another important perspective. I love keeping it real, and this subject is no different. The reality is we sometimes walk into things before we are equipped with the tools and wisdom to make godly decisions. I want to speak to you, virtuous woman, who put on the ring before you knew you were a virtuous woman—before your spiritual eyes were open to know what you should accept and should let pass by. I want to set you free through these words, "The Lord has not abandoned you and cast you away because you didn't wait on Him to bring you His choice." So many times, we forget the sovereignty of our Father. He knew that choice before you made it and guess what? Now that you know who you are in Him, He can get the glory. The world will tell you to leave that man and call it quits, and many times that mindset gets carried over to the minds of believers. Maybe you are asking yourself why the Lord would ask you to stay in something He never ordained. But who is to say He didn't? We have to remember that His ways are so much higher than ours.

> "THE CHOICE YOU MADE DID NOT STOP THE CALL OR THE PLANS THAT GOD HAS FOR YOUR LIFE."

A great example of the reckless love of our Father is the Book of Hosea. If you have never read that story and you are currently struggling in your marriage, I strongly suggest you read it. Hosea is about a man, not just a man, a prophet, who was married to a woman who kept having affairs and did unspeakable things that most of us would walk away from. But the Lord kept telling Hosea to go get her. I am not telling you what you should do, but I do want to encourage you that the Lord can do the impossible. I know so many women who have been made to feel like there is no hope in their marriage, but I want you to know that is a lie. Give your marriage to God and watch Him get the glory. The choice you made did not stop the call or the plans that God has for your life.

Waiting on God can cause you to go through things you would not have gone through, but it is not a forfeit to the plans He has for you. In fact, those tests and trials you are going through in your marriage are purifying you. The ones telling you to call it quits are one of two people.

This is usually someone who is not married or someone who called it quits on their own marriage. That truth is not for everyone. However, virtuous woman, that truth is for you. If you have been asking the Lord for wisdom in your marriage, let me encourage you to first be still. Listen for His small voice to lead you, and if you don't hear anything, do nothing. I would like to take the time to point out the benefit of waiting on God. Sometimes when you do not wait on the Lord and you choose, it will cause you to run into many problems. I have counseled many couples. The main issue that arises is the unsaved spouse struggles to understand the commitment to the call. That can cause a major wedge in the marriage. Being married to an unsaved spouse can cause obstacles while you are pursuing your call. There have also been times when the unsaved spouse became jealous of the spouse for walking in their calling. In pleasing the Lord, our spouse becomes a major priority. When we have an unsaved spouse, they become our ministry, and a lot of our focus has to be shifted towards them. Not to say that the work is not beneficial, it's just to say that it can cause a delay in the progress of the calling we have. When thinking about marriage, I can't express how important it is to seek God and allow him to do the choosing.

When you wait on the Lord, it becomes two people joined together to help one another walk in His purpose. There is no competition between two believers walking toward the same purpose. When your spouse is also a believer, they push you forward in your calling and strengthen you. A God-ordained relationship is one where when one is down the other can pull them up. A godly marriage looks like peace, and when there are trying times, both of you pull together and overcome. That's not to say that there are no issues with a godly relationship, but it makes things a lot easier than with a nonbeliever. The Bible makes it clear that we should be equally yoked in relationships. I encourage you, women of God to truly wait on the Lord and let Him give you the desires of your heart. Whether you know it or not, you are a virtuous woman and you are worth the wait.

SUPPLICATION

Dear Heavenly Father,

I want to thank you this day for living on the inside of me. I want to thank you for your Holy Spirit that empowers me to do anything and all things. Today, Lord, I thank you that you are the center of my life. Lord, you know my desire to have the character of the virtuous woman that your word speaks about. I thank you for giving me the tools necessary to be the wife that is pleasing to you. Thank you for healing me from all past hurts and traumas so I can walk in the fullness of who you have called me to be. Thank you that in my marriage I cover my husband and choose to be the woman of God, in my home, you desire me to be. Thank you, Holy Spirit, for giving me all the tools to be the wife of noble character. Thank you for taking my imperfections and empowering me to do what on my own I can't do. In Jesus' name.

AFFIRMATION

I am no longer a victim but always an overcomer.

I do not allow my past hurts to determine the wife I am in my marriage.

I am more than a conqueror.

I overcome all the hindrances in my life that have the potential to cause my marriage to struggle.

I am a wife of noble character.

I am no longer broken, but I am made whole in the image of Christ.

In my singleness, I pursue Christ.

In my marriage, I make Christ the center.

I find my worth and value in Christ and not material things, education, economic status, or relationship status.

I lay down my life daily for Christ so He can get the glory in all that I do.

The Holy Spirit is my strength and giving up is never an option for me.

I always trust God with impossible situations in my life.

Today I choose the character of Christ, which will lead me to be a wife of noble character.

APPLICATION

1. If you are married, set a particular time every day and create a space where you and your husband cover one another in prayer.

    Time: _____

    Location: _____

2. If you are single, make taking yourself out on a date a priority at least once a month.

    Date Night: _____

3. If you are married, pick a day, at least once a week, where you unplug from all electronics and be totally into one another.

    Day: _____

4. Before the beginning of every day, spend time in prayer and in the word of God. Your relationship with Him is the foundation for every area in your life.

5. Read Proverbs 31 and write down the qualities that describe the character of the virtuous woman. Highlight areas where you would like to improve and work on those areas daily.

    _____
    _____
    _____
    _____
    _____
    _____
    _____
    _____
    _____

REFLECTIONS

Take a moment and write down your thoughts

_____

_____

_____

_____

_____

_____

_____

_____

_____

_____

_____

_____

_____

_____

_____

_____

_____

_____

_____

_____

_____

_____

_____

_____

_____

_____

_____

_____

_____

ABOUT THE AUTHOR

Temecka Smith has one goal in mind, to be the hands and feet of Jesus. The hats she wears are many in number, but preaching the unadulterated truth, in her eyes, is the most important. She serves as the associate pastor of **Good Samaritan Center of Hope** in Knoxville, Tennessee, where she has labored for nine years. She has a passion for seeing lives changed, which is made evident as she is the founder of her international ministry **Real Life, Real Issues**. In using her powerful testimony, Temecka travels to reach people from all walks of life, from the unchurched all the way to the leaders who are in need of healing themselves, in an environment where they can "take off their masks." **Real Life, Real Issues** was birthed out of her home over ten years ago and has now grown to be a cooperative fellowship that meets once a month to love on the lost. The heart she has for the abandoned, lost, and rejected comes from walking miles in those very shoes. Temecka has been in corporate America for over twenty years. Because of the heart, she has for people, she has found it hard to leave due to the amount of ministry opportunities that take place within the marketplace. Temecka and her husband, George, are proud parents and grandparents, who keep their hearts full. She and her husband make their home in Knoxville, Tennessee. Her goal is to take God's truth to hurting people and show them how He can create beauty from ashes as he did with her own life. Temecka truly has a servant's heart and a trumpet set to her mouth to sound the alarm in this generation.

CONTACT INFORMATION

Email Address: Smitem444@gmail.com

Website:

SOCIAL MEDIA

Twitter:

Facebook Page: @Temecka Smith

Instagram: @Temecka Smith

BUILT IN THE FIRE
Sharon P. Jones

"Strength and honour are her clothing; and she shall
rejoice in time to come."
Proverbs 31:25 (KJV)

When I got married, my ministry title position instantly became "Pastor's wife" or "First Lady." I was excited about this new chapter in my life. I'd been serving at my home church and learned so much from being in ministry for the previous fifteen years. I was ready to apply what I learned. I showed up ready to serve. Just as important, I was prepared to serve in the kingdom of God with the love of my life! Many of the members each had a different idea of who I should be, what I should do and what I should wear, as well as why I don't wear a hat with my outfit. I generally assisted when I was needed. Sometimes, I graciously honored requests for my presence or assistance and other times declined.

Over time, I began to feel overwhelmed. I felt like the members were trying to make me do what they "thought" I should do as the church's first lady. After much prayer, the pastor determined that I would oversee the women's ministry.

What I experienced was not what I expected. In the process of moving forward with the women's ministry, there was low cooperation and a lack of support. After about three years, I decided to stop pouring my energy, where there was no support. The very last event with this women's group was the holiday dinner celebration at a local restaurant. The event was planned timely at a restaurant that the women chose, and no one showed up. When I followed up with the women to ask what happened, each one said they heard the meeting was canceled. I did not plan or schedule any more activities for the women's ministry. I reallocated my energy. The timing was perfect as that was when my son (at the time three years old) started playing sports.

The women in the church began to gather occasionally for dinner and to have meetings. One time, they even had a shut-in. I was not invited nor made aware of these gatherings. The annual women's day service was also scheduled and planned. I was not made aware but was expected to be present. One year, in particular, Women's Day was scheduled on a weekend that posed a conflict due to a holiday as well as a scheduling conflict for me, due to plans already scheduled months in advance. This information was presented to the planning committee, and the response was, "We always celebrate women's day on the fourth Sunday in May." I did not attend. That weekend was my daughter's high school graduation. I had family in town to celebrate my daughter. My mom had come to church with us Sunday morning, and we were meeting with other family members that afternoon. We attended morning service and had dinner and fellowship at the church. After dinner, my mom, my children, and I left for the other scheduled family activities. Interestingly enough, the following year, I was unable to attend women's day due to my son (who was three years old at the time) having a fever of 106 F. As I recall, there was a lot of conflict regarding the planning that year. There would be many more incidents to occur over the years, but I'd already checked out of the women's ministry. I was over it.

It is not my intent to spend time on details about who or what kept division among the women. I want to share what God did in me and for me in this process. There was a process for sure. I was disappointed, hurt, and angry. I was appalled that I would experience these things in church. The ministry would encounter another year of low cooperation and low support and low participation. Each year the support was diminishing. As I was reflecting and evaluating, I realized I had lost focus. In the process of God rebuilding me, I had to go through the fire to get to where God wanted me to be.

THE BUILDING PROCESS

In the process of being rebuilt, it did not feel good. I would go through many emotions because I felt unappreciated and disrespected. I would experience hurt, anger, and discouragement. What I learned and experienced in ministry, I felt I would share at my new church home with my new church family. As a congregation, we were a working church. We were doing regular outreach as well as our regular services and Bible studies, revivals, etc. Each week we were providing food and clothing to the community. I saw unlimited opportunities to serve and for the church to be a light in the community.

THE REBUILDING PROCESS DOESN'T ALWAYS FEEL GOOD

I was disappointed because I thought I was doing a good thing (wanting to see the church excel). The real disappointment and hurt were not being received or accepted by the women in the church. The underlying issue is that there were unresolved issues with rejection. I continued to pray about this until the root of the rejection was identified. My first experience with rejection was in elementary school. I did not attend the local elementary school in the neighborhood. I was bussed to a school in another neighborhood. In this school, the student population was multicultural and varied ethnicities. Some students did not play with me because of my skin color and made that reason known. Some students did not want to sit next to me at lunch for this same reason. When moving from classroom to classroom, we as students were paired in twos and walked together holding hands, and some of my classmates did not want to hold my hand. As a little girl, I most certainly did not know how to process that, so I didn't.

Anger began to set in. I was angry because I felt betrayed. I felt betrayed by my fellow co-laborers. I felt betrayed by my fellow Christian sisters. I did not expect to experience what I'd experience in the church. I thought that we were on the same team. I could not believe that Christians could behave this way. This experience was so contrary to what I've experienced in other Christian settings. I felt I was betrayed by the very people I was called to serve. I should have not allowed my anger to grow in this situation as, in retrospect, the congregation were strangers to me and vice versa. We did not officially meet until I was introduced as the first lady. None of us had the option of choosing one another. Even with that, what happened to the fruit of "love" as mentioned in the book of Galatians in the Bible that we all read and use as a guide for our life? The word and act of "Love" are mentioned so many times in the Bible. According to the word, Love is not an option. Love is a commandment. As I reflect on that experience, I wonder if the love I was expecting from others was void due to how I was really feeling about myself. It was time for me to deal with the anger I was feeling within myself. At times, we think it's easier to blame others for things we don't want to address......But guess what? Eventually, that "thing" has to be dealt with. Sometimes it comes with fire. In reflection of the situation, in retrospect, I could have done relational building activities which would have allowed us to get acquainted with one another and gathered feedback from the women to determine the direction the women's ministry would proceed. Over the next few years, the women's ministry was not progressing in accordance with the church vision, thus creating a hindrance in the ministry. After careful consideration, fasting and praying, the pastor made a decision to call a special meeting and release the flock. Each member was prayed for and released from the church. Eight weeks later, the church would experience a re-boot and we started with two new families who joined the church. New members joined us as well. My husband and I are still serving together in ministry.

All of the feelings I was experiencing surrounding this situation caused me to become discouraged. As I wallowed in discouragement, I realized I lost

> **"I DID NOT EXPECT TO EXPERIENCE WHAT I'D EXPERIENCE IN THE CHURCH."**

focus. I believed God had a purpose and a plan for my life, but what was it? During this period of examination and exploration, I would pray, fellowship with other women in ministry and other pastor's wives. As I spent more quality time with God, I remember this scripture, "Cast your cares on the Lord and he will sustain you, he will never let the righteous be shaken" (Psalm 55:22 NIV). Also, Isaiah 41:10 (NIV) reads, "So do not fear, for I am with you; do not be dismayed, for I am your God. I will strengthen you and help you; I will uphold you with my righteous right hand." There would be many more scriptures, but these specific two provided great relief when I was feeling discouraged. I did not expect to experience what I'd experience in the church.

One Saturday in November, I attended a conference for women in leadership. The women were either senior pastors, pastor's wives, or women with a ministry/organization. The women were kind and supportive. The fellowship was sweet. In that very atmosphere, I heard the Lord give me nuggets of information and instructions to move forward with the women's ministry. A few months later, when I would share with my husband what God spoke to me, he encouraged me to go forth. The following November would be the birth of Women on the Front Line Global Outreach Ministries. The vision of WOTFL is to Transform Lives and Impact generations.

The mission of WOTFL is to encourage, empower and educate women of current and future generations to live a victorious life in Christ according to the scripture 3 John 2, "Beloved, I wish above all things that thou mayest prosper and be in health, even as thy soul prospereth" (KJV).

> "CAST YOUR CARES ON THE LORD AND HE WILL SUSTAIN YOU, HE WILL NEVER LET THE RIGHTEOUS BE SHAKEN"

The mission is carried out in three strategies:

I. Kingdom Living Series - Establishing identity and purpose through Vision Board workshops, goal setting, and coaching
II. Kingdom Business Series - Providing information and resources for financial empowering using kingdom principles
III. Kingdom Transformation Series - Providing life-changing information through the Word of God via conferences and seminars

Each year WOTFL hosts an event for each strategy. The month of November 2020 was the seventh year for the Kingdom Transformation Series via the Kingdom Takeover Conference. Every year, each fellowship experiences an increase. I give all glory and honor to God for this.

THE VICTORY

Proverbs 31:25 states, "Strength and honour are her clothing, and she shall rejoice in time to come." Strength and honour listed as her clothing refer to her spiritual attributes and her character, not clothing garments. This woman lives her life by wearing these qualities. The qualities are reflective of how she presents herself at home and in the marketplace. This description also reflects her behavior and how she governs herself around other individuals.

While in my process, I remember I am "fearfully and wonderfully made (Psalm 139:14)." I also know and remember that "I can do all things through Christ who strengthens me" (Philippians 4:13). I do realize that God loves me! He loved us so much that He gave the life of His only Son (John 3:16).

Let's fast-forward to the women's ministry in 2020. In 2014, the new women's ministry launched in November. This year the seventh annual conference took place. We had to adapt due to COVID-19 and host a virtual conference.

With the current and continuous help from the Lord, I was able to stand firm in my identity. I realize that God created me for a purpose. It doesn't matter who agrees or disagrees. God is in control and has the final say. This is confirmed in 1 Peter 2:9, "But ye are a chosen generation, a royal priesthood, a holy nation, a peculiar people; that ye should shew forth the praises of him who hath called you out of darkness into his marvelous light;" I stood firm in my faith and did not waiver as written in James 1:12, "Blessed is the man that endureth temptation: for when he is tried, he shall receive the crown of life, which the Lord hath promised to them that love him" and Romans 8:18, "For I reckon that the sufferings of this present time are not worthy to be compared with the glory which shall be revealed in us." Lastly, I had to become bold in truth as stated in 2 Timothy 1:7, "For God hath not given us the spirit of fear; but of power, and of love, and of a sound mind."

IN CLOSING

In my experience, I took what other people said about me, felt about me, or thought about me and allowed it to be my truth. That false truth caused me to get off focus. The lesson learned for me is to stay focused. I'm learning to stay focused on what's important to me, my life and my purpose. Some days, I'm more successful than others. It's still a process for me. I feel victorious because I have victory in Jesus Christ! I find that as I stay focused, I am least distracted by the unimportant things. I have also made self-care a priority (that's another chapter for another time). As this year is closing, I am grateful for making it this far. I wait with great expectations for great things for next year. God is still building me, and for that I'm grateful.

SUPPLICATION

Dear Holy Father,

I lift up mine eyes to the hills, from where my help comes from. I Thank you for being my help. I praise you, honor you and glorify you. I bless your holy name. I thank you for being the lifter of my head. As I go forth today, I thank you for ordering my steps. I thank you for guiding my thoughts, words, and deeds so that all I do will glorify you. Create in me a clean heart and renew a right spirit within me. Forgive me for my sins, trespasses and shortcomings and strengthen me to forgive others for the same. I ask, Father, that you remove all hindrances that keep me from walking with you and I thank you for giving me ears to hear you. I thank you for what you've done, what you're doing now and what you shall do, and I give you all the glory, honor and praise. In the mighty name of Jesus, I pray…. Amen.

After the supplication, list three things you are grateful for:

1. I am grateful for_____

_____

2. I am grateful for _____

_____

3. I am grateful for _____

_____

AFFIRMATIONS

1.   God loves me. I love and respect myself.

     Bible reference: *John 3:16 (KJV) "For God so loved the world, that he gave his only begotten Son, that whosoever believeth in him should not perish, but have everlasting life."*

2.   I am transforming. My mind is renewed.

     Bible reference: *Romans 12:1-2 "I beseech you therefore, brethren, by the mercies of God, that ye present your bodies a living sacrifice, holy, acceptable unto God, which is your reasonable service. 2 And be not conformed to this world: but be ye transformed by the renewing of your mind, that ye may prove what is that good, and acceptable, and perfect, will of God.*

3.   I only compare myself to myself. The power to change lies within me.

     Bible reference: *Philippians 4:13 (KJV), "I can do all things through Christ which strengtheneth me."*

APPLICATION

In the process of examining myself, I realized the feelings I experienced in church was tied to other unresolved hurt, anger, and disappointments. While hurting, I reflected on previous hurts and determined that those feelings were buried and not addressed. The individuals who inflicted the hurt may not be accessible or alive to confront, but the issue still must be addressed. Let's try this exercise:

Think back to your childhood….. Think back to an incident where you were disappointed or hurt. Now answer the following:

Describe the incident where you were disappointed, hurt, or angry:

_____
_____
_____
_____

Who was the violator (person that caused the hurt, disappointment, or anger)?

_____

_____

How did this incident make you feel? Be honest with yourself.

_____
_____
_____
_____
_____

Has the violator been confronted? _____

Has the issue been addressed by you with the violator?
_____

What would you say to the violator right now if they were standing right in front of you? Feel free to continue on another sheet of paper, notebook, or journal.

_____
_____
_____
_____
_____
_____

Use this same exercise with old, more recent, or current unresolved issues using the same questions

Now go to your Bible and look up the following scriptures:

1 Peter 2:9 (write what is says):

_____

_____

_____

Romans 8:18 (write what is says):

_____

_____

_____

Philippians 4:13 (write what is says):

_____

_____

_____

2 Timothy 1:7 (write what is says):

_____

_____

_____

In my experience, I took what other people said about me and allowed it to be my truth. The truth of the matter is that I am who God says I am. The aforementioned scriptures are reminders. In the exercise with the scriptures, I want the scripture to be written so that while writing, you will have a better idea of God's thoughts toward you. I've had to do it for myself and still do. God indeed does have a plan for your life as the Bible reminds us in Jeremiah 29:11 (NIV), "For I know the plans I have for you," declares the Lord, "plans to prosper you and not to harm you, plans to give you hope and a future." As I read and studied the Bible and prayed, similar incidents over the years did not affect me. I choose to always believe what the Bible says.

REFLECTIONS

Take a moment and write down your thoughts

_____

_____

_____

_____

_____

_____

_____

_____

_____

_____

_____

_____

_____

_____

_____

_____

_____

_____

_____

_____

_____

_____

_____

ABOUT THE AUTHOR

Lady Sharon Jones is the CEO of Queendominion Enterprises, LLC (established 2011) and Executive Director and Founder of Women on the Front-Line Global Outreach Ministries (established November 2013), where the vision is transforming lives and impacting generations. WOTFL's mission is to encourage, empower and educate women of all generations to live a victorious life in Christ according to Bible scripture 3 John 2, "Beloved, I wish above all things that thou mayest prosper and be in health, even as thy soul prospereth." Lady Sharon is a New York native who has made Atlanta her home.

Sharon has earned a bachelor's degree from Queens College (Flushing, NY), Master of Science Degree (Public Administration Concentration) from Central Michigan University, and a Graduate Certificate in Project Management from Capella University. Sharon also received a Diploma from Georgia Certified Life Coach Academy.

In addition, she has received certificates of completion for "When Leaders Lead" taught by the late Bishop Earl Paulk from the Cathedral of the Holy Spirit and Master Life Discipleship Series.

Sharon served in the U.S. Army Reserves over 20 years and completed service at the Officer rank of Captain. She has over 20 years of experience working with the Department of Human Resources/Services in New York and Georgia and is a former Business Analyst with the State of Georgia. She currently serves as a board member with Pillar of Fire Christian Ministries, Biloxi, MS, Pathway Christian Ministries, in Atlanta, GA, and formerly with The Elect Lady Ministries, McDonough, GA. Sharon is a Certified Life Coach and best-selling author.

When not working or serving in ministry, Sharon enjoys reading and spending time with family. Lady Sharon, the wife, mother, sister, daughter, and friend aspires to live her life according to God's promise in 3 John 2.

CONTACT INFORMATION
Email Address: wotflglobal@gmail.com

SOCIAL MEDIA

Facebook Page: @wotflglobal, @Sharon Jones Author

Instagram: @wotflglobal

BUILT TO LAST
Barbara Beckley

31:27 (KJV) She looketh well to the ways of her household, and eateth not the bread of idleness. Proverbs 31:27

When a house, building, or anything is built, you have to think about the foundation. When you are building, you have to make sure it can stand the storms and changes in the environment, or it can fall, be destroyed, or could cause increasing problems for the owner and others around the building. You would need to ask the experts who handle construction to make sure you have a safe location, the supplies to lay the foundation, and insight into what challenges might arise in the timeframe of building.

You must consider who will be a part of the team to make the project and location come together to get the best results of having your property completed.   There is also the maintenance and the insurance needed to ensure your building and property are protected and enhanced when required.

PSALM 18:2

THE LORD IS MY ROCK AND MY FORTRESS AND MY DELIVERER, MY GOD, MY ROCK, IN WHOM I TAKE REFUGE, MY SHIELD, AND THE HORN OF MY SALVATION, MY STRONGHOLD.

Just as a building need a solid foundation to support its structure. We must have a strong foundation to support every aspect of our lives so that we may keep healthy and hold up during storms.   Everyone comes from a different family environment that raises them to either be valuable contributors or unproductive within society. In spite of our upbringing, there comes the point in life where you have to make choices that promote a healthy lifestyle and cultivate a better version of yourself. I had to make a choice when I experienced an event that took away my choice. I decided to say the word NO, but my abuser thought it meant yes. I was sexually abused, and my voice did not matter at that time. I felt ashamed, fearful, my esteem was low, and I felt as though the whole foundation of my life was shattered. I thought it was built to last, but an outsider came into my property and tore up the foundation, challenging my self-worth. I wanted to go into self-pity mode and make myself believe that I could not move forward with my goals and dreams because of the strength taken by the storm.

Before I was about to give up hope and give up on the move forward, I remembered my aunt's words a few years ago, "Anything you go through in life that is challenging and hits your heart, the Bible will have the answers for you. Still, you have to believe what it says in the word, NOT just read it." I had my Bible in my closet, and I asked myself, "What will it hurt to start the process of looking for answers to help you from a deep hole?" I flipped to the back of the Bible to look up the area where I struggled. I would pick topics about hurting and helpless individuals and look at stories and scriptures about building a foundation.

I knew this was not me, but I did not fight it. In most of the readings, I read about building on a strong foundation of God's word, listening, and getting instructions to rebuild and maintain. I told myself I needed to make sure I found every scripture which pertained to a foundation. The inner voice told me there were some steps I needed to take to rebuild my foundation and make it healthy.

There are three main points needed to help put the building blocks together to secure a strong foundation. 1) Prayer, 2) Studying and hearing the word of God, and 3) Stating Affirmations. They are the tools to help start and keep maintenance within you.

First, we must pray, not just talking to God and asking for his direction, strength, and gifts. We must also listen to what he has to say. He will give you the steps to build a relationship with

2 TIMOTHY 3:16-17

ALL SCRIPTURE IS BREATHED OUT BY GOD AND PROFITABLE FOR TEACHING, FOR REPROOF, FOR CORRECTION, AND FOR TRAINING IN RIGHTEOUSNESS, THAT THE MAN OF GOD MAY BE COMPETENT, EQUIPPED FOR EVERY GOOD WORK.

him to know and understand who you are. Just as we communicate with family, friends, and associates, we have to dialog with God. Often, we give God a laundry list of items we want to be done in our lives and sit back and wait for them to come to pass. Still, we miss that part that God wants to build the foundation with us and needs us to listen to what he feels is best in our lives to reach the next level and create the brick that lays at the bottom. Sometimes, what we ask may not be what God has in store; in

fact, it can be the total opposite of what we want instead of what we need. We might question why, but God is always looking at the bigger picture. We have to trust and believe it's best for our foundation. I would have never thought the same person who was bullied and sexually assaulted would become a professional speaker and a three-time best-selling author. Still, it happened when I took the step to build a foundation and trusted the process.

The second step is studying and following the Word of God; you will hear from him through the scriptures and stories within the Bible. It's a map for your life, and it leads you to the other bricks to lay a firm foundation. When you have to build or put together maybe a furniture piece, it comes with instructions. This is the same with our lives. The Bible is our instruction guide to put the pieces together. When we read the stories in the Word, we find many examples of what we might be dealing with within our world, and they give us hope that there is a way to move forward and become stronger and have a purpose.

You might hear people state that words are powerful because when you say them out loud and believe them, they can come to pass in your life. It works both ways, good and bad, so you have to know what the living words are saying to you to breathe life into your foundation to stand tall and secure.

The third block is affirmations to keep you aware of who you are and what you are becoming. Again, if we know words are living, we have to allow them to build in us to trust and believe who we are. Then, we can conquer our past.

"BUILDING FAITH COMES BY HEARING THE WORD"

Building faith comes by hearing the word and making sure you believe in who you are in God. You can say, "I am amazing. I am smart. I am worthy. I am loved, etc." These are a few you could begin with to meditate and stay in front of the mirror. You need to create repetitions so they can get into your mind, heart, and soul. Eventually, you will begin to speak them automatically. As a reminder, words are living. If something is living, you nurture it, and it will grow. When you believe you are smart, you continue to learn every day until it grows more inside of you. Once the seed is planted, water it by speaking it out into the world until it's what you genuinely believe what you are saying about yourself.

As I look back as one who was sexually abused, trying to figure out how to move forward, trying to believe in myself, and build a trust factor, especially when it came to a relationship with men, I know something in me was broken but fixable. It took me telling myself, "I need a foundation to build" and get rid of the words playing in my head, "You asked for it. You are so stupid. Why would anyone want to be around you? You bring bad luck to people."

It took finding my way to the Bible and looking up and believing who I was in God's eyes and not my own. How is your foundation? Are you speaking life or death? Have the storms in your life taken over, uprooting your foundation?

It is essential to take inventory to determine if you need to call a contractor to maintain your foundation or build another one that will withstand anything that comes.

I knew I committed once I began believing in myself after my vicious storm came. I might have hurt physically and mentally, but surviving was the key. I had another chance to take my unique talents and skills to impact others. Also, I was able to tell my story of stepping stones of strengths, to have a connection with others and give hope.

Appreciate and enjoy your uniqueness that brings the special gifts and talents you have to help build the foundation of life.

SUPPLICATION

Father, I thank you in the name of Jesus for giving me the awareness to understand that you are my foundation, and anything that comes my way cannot be torn down because you are my strength in all the corners of my life. You give me the wisdom, knowledge, and capability to know what steps I need to take. It is your word that has built my foundation to enable me to withstand the storms of life. In your truth, I gain the understanding as it consistently reminds me of who I am in you. I will keep your words upon my lips so that I will never forget your thoughts towards me and the foundation on which I stand. Also, you gave me the ability to take the storms and hurricanes in my life and know they are stepping stones of strength to remind myself that I need to continue to thank you for everything you do for me and others.

Matthew 7:24-27 – "Everyone then who hears these words of mine and does them will be like a wise man who built his house on the rock. And the rain fell, and the floods came, and the winds blew and beat on that house, but it did not fall because it had been founded on the rock. And everyone who hears these words of mine and does not do them will be like a foolish man who built his house on the sand. And the rain fell, and the floods came, and the winds blew and beat against that house, and it fell, and great was the fall of it."

Matthew 7:25 – "And the rain fell, and the floods came, and the winds blew and beat on that house, but it did not fall, because it had been founded on the rock."

Proverbs 16:9 – "The heart of man plans his way, but the Lord establishes his steps."

AFFIRMATION

I believe in my purpose.
I have a solid foundation in my life.
I am more than enough.
I shall not let negative words define me.
I am more than a conqueror.
I rebuke any storm that will try to destroy my foundation.
I shall NOT live in fear of others.
I am special.
I am unique because God has plans for me to create an impact with my uniqueness.

APPLICATION

Help To Build Your Foundation

Sticks, Straw, or Bricks! When I think of building a foundation, it takes me back to my childhood days when I heard the three little pigs' story. Each pig took off and wanted to live and be independent. The pigs decided they needed a place to call their home and make sure they were safe and secure, but two of the three pigs wanted to rush in building their house. They picked items around them, not thinking things through or paying attention to the type of supplies and tools they were using to build.

When the wolf came around (the storms of life) and blew down the straw and sticks house, the foundation could not withstand the storm (hurricanes or life challenges). But the third pig took his time and built his house out of brick to assure the foundation would hold through the storms.

You want to make sure you take the steps and obtain the tools to start building your foundation or keep the maintenance upon the foundation you already have in place.

In the following statement, you want to identify what makes a good foundation and what it will take to impact positively. What do you think the Lord might say to you about how to collect your tools? First, write down all the items you want to see within your building of life?

What type of people are around you? What values are you incorporating? What kind of boundaries are you setting up?

_____

_____

_____

_____

Look at what type of (challenges or oppositions) you can expect to come your way and know the solutions or how to handle them.

To overcome my challenges, I will (solution):

_____

_____

_____

_____

Overcoming Scripture: Write scriptures from the Word of God that you can have as a reminder regarding the storms of life you experience that will make you stronger and not give up the fight.

_____
_____
_____
_____

Choose the tools you will use to build your solid foundation or continue to evaluate the foundation you already have. To build a physical foundation, you would probably need brick, cement, a hammer, nails, etc. For your spiritual foundation, you will need the Word of God, prayer, daily meditation, studying the Word, and other faith-based individuals supporting you.

Find a person who can be an accountability partner to assure you are using the tools and staying on your plan of building your structure.

_____
_____
_____
_____

Look up as many scriptures concerning foundation. Keep them near you as a reminder of why it's essential to have that foundation built.

_____
_____
_____
_____

REFLECTIONS

Take a moment and write down your thoughts

_____

_____

_____

_____

_____

_____

_____

_____

_____

_____

_____

_____

_____

_____

_____

_____

_____

_____

_____

_____

_____

_____

_____

_____

_____

_____

_____

_____

_____

ABOUT THE AUTHOR

Barbara Beckley is a professional keynote speaker, a three-time Amazon best-selling author, a purpose strategist, and social media personality. She is the founder and CEO of the Diamond Factor, LLC. She empowers people to understand their PPD (Purpose, Passion, and Drive), especially women, to help them overcome their challenges to shine like a diamond in their business and personal life. For the past nine years, with her communication and leadership skills, Barbara worked her way up to becoming a Program Quality Director, providing educational opportunities for over 5500 potential clients. In addition, she has over 30+ years' experience working within the Commercial Insurance Industry as a broker and mentor. Barbara offers services including webinars training, one on one coaching, and keynote presentation concerning personal development. Also, to help increase visibility, she does interviews to promote a person's business and/or special causes, including image and content coaching. You can find Barbara on social media, where she loves connecting and sharing tips and strategies on all things concerning your purpose and growth.

CONTACT INFORMATION

Email Address: diamondfactorexperience@gmail.com

Website:

SOCIAL MEDIA

Twitter:

Facebook: https://www.facebook.com/groups/DiamondFactorBB/

Instagram:

BEING A VOICE TO THE VOICELESS
LaWanna Bradford

She stretches out her hand to the poor; yes, she reaches forth her hands to the needy.
Proverbs 31:20

The virtuous woman stretches out her hand to the poor and needy, which addresses her charitable heart. In earlier passages, we understand that she not only works for her household, but she takes the proceeds and then reinvests them. This passage speaks to the generosity and compassion that she extends to those in need. It denotes that this gesture is not just a one-time occurrence, but reflects that she is committed to meeting the needs and bridging the divide. Across the world, we have a need for our virtuous women to rise up and stretch out their hands. Here in the United States there are so many who have lost their jobs, businesses, and loved ones to this catastrophic pandemic. As such, many never envisioned themselves being on the sidelines of life, facing a state of financial and health panic, with a hand humbly opened, saying, "Help me."

As I look around at the tsunamic change that has enveloped the entire world, I feel a sense of heightened gratitude for my physical, mental, emotional, and financial well-being. I wonder how many of us are willing and able to use our positions of leadership, authority, and influence to serve as a catalyst to impact and better society. When I use the term 'society,' I see it as more than the global reference we often give it. Society can be that neighborhood that you live in, your church, or the school your children attend. It is that lived-life community that you experience within your sphere of influence. God moves and flows through us and connects us within the social fabric of life. When we surrender and allow the Spirit to lead, the universe begins to shift and bend to our prayers and acts of faith. As we move with authority, establishing dominion around us, this is when we receive confirmation that we are influencers, leaders, and change agents. This is the time when our voice gives rise to the unheard cries of the marginalized.

During 2007-2008, I became one of the marginalized. Prior to the economic mortgage crisis, I was basking in abundance and increase. Suddenly, I, along with thousands of others, found myself the victim of poor Wall Street decisions and constructs. It appeared that I had toppled from grace and favor to a person no longer seen as worthy by those who held the purse strings. With the flow of income in question, I was treated differently, even by my so-called friends. My essence of being had not changed. I was still the same person that I was the day before. Yet, when I walked into the bank, I was treated as less than, and my accounts were changed or placed in a lower status. My business creditors pounced on me like vultures and demanded all payments immediately with the threat of lawsuits if I failed to pay. The landscape had definitely changed, and my face was analogous to "not our kind of client." They were not looking at my character or my financial history. Where was the favor? The banks did not acknowledge the billions of government bail-out funds they had received and only sank their teeth deeper into my dwindling bank accounts. It had become a paradoxical dog-eat-dog world; they had received assistance on the backs of our tax paying dollars, but refused to extend their hand to me, a long-standing client.

Today, so many have been adversely impacted and traumatized by a situation that is beyond their control. These individuals can often become more discouraged and feel lost because they are spinning in what appears to be a cesspool of never-ending chaos. As countless have fallen over the edge into this financial abyss, I wonder what I can do. I know how this feels and like the virtuous woman, I want to be one who extends her hands to those in need. The entire world is groaning under the ills this pandemic has brought; therefore, how can we see those in need and hear their cries and turn with a callous heart? Everyone has a story. We cannot bring prejudgment to the table since we never know from where they have come, or what their financial situation may have been.

"There but for the grace of God, go I," is a mid-sixteenth century quote from John Bradford that I often reflect upon. Although I was at a place where I had to make a decision between keeping health insurance or the lights on, I still had a roof over my head and food in my belly. During my dark hour, I have to admit I had my earthly angel guiding and teaching me how to make the right choices and navigate, what was then, my new normal. When we feel pressed and are faced with life's upheavals, we need people around us who will gird us up and give us hope and encouragement.

GALATIANS 6:2 - CARRY EACH OTHER'S BURDENS, AND IN THIS WAY YOU WILL FULFILL THE LAW OF CHRIST."

The need, as the virtuous woman recognized, is more than praying and standing in the gap. Matthew 25:35-40 recognizes a giving heart, and tells us, "In as much as you have done for the least of my brothers, you have done it to me." It is an active work that we must do to reach out to humanity and say that we are here. I believe that is what the virtuous woman was doing. In all of her gains and fiscal stewardship, the scripture tells us that she was conscientious, invested, and made sound decisions. From her increase, she was doing more and creating more wealth for herself and her family, yet she did not selfishly say, "This is all that I have" and, "life is all about me." She refused to turn deaf ears to the cry or close her eyes to the hurt, the pain, and the suffering. She instead said, "I do see, and I do hear. I will lend my hand to the poor and to those in need."

2 CORINTHIANS 9:7

"EACH OF YOU SHOULD GIVE WHAT YOU HAVE DECIDED IN OUR HEART TO GIVE, NOT RELUCTANTLY OR UNDER COMPULSION, BECAUSE GOD LOVES A CHEERFUL GIVER."

When we reflect on our leadership, authority, and influence, to not get involved, and to silence our voice is not what God has called us to do. These are the moments where we leverage our influence and leadership to create partnerships and strategic relationships that will enable us to go into communities, implement initiatives, and provide hope and support.

It is not always about trading our time for a dollar. Sometimes we are trading our time for the enhancement of someone's life. That is invaluable. You can't put a price tag on someone's life, on someone's well-being and quality of life. That is priceless. When we trade our time as the virtuous woman did, our acts of kindness demonstrate that there are people who are out here who care and who can make a difference. When we think about the mental, spiritual, and physical well-being of another, there is a role we can play. There is something that we can do.

If you don't know what to do, sometimes you just need to pause and assess the land and see where the laborers are needed. We can get so caught in the "I need to pray about it" mindset, that we become trapped in our own self-professed holiness. Sometimes it is as simple as saying, "I don't have to pray about it. I just need to open up my eyes and ears and hear and see and then decide to make a difference." Deciding to be that image of Christ is saying "Yes" to being our brother's keeper. We do have a responsibility to humanity. I believe the virtuous woman was demonstrating that in her increase and abundance, she was able to turn and say, "Because of this, I am going to be obedient and have a love walk. I am going to look and see where I may be able to extend my hand to those who are poor and in need." The extension of her hand represents that she is holding something for them that they can take to help them, to encourage them, to feed them mentally, physically, spiritually, emotionally, and perhaps, even financially.

We were not called to sit on the sidelines. In such a time as this, women are being called to rise up mightily. Even when we get beyond this, we should never forget from where we have come, or get so caught up in our abundant living that we turn a deaf ear and a blind eye to those in need. Let us continue to stretch our hands to the poor and needy and exercise our voice to spotlight the pains of the world. We can be the spark to light a mighty fire and create a massive inferno of change.

SUPPLICATION

Father, I thank you for Your guidance and the examples you have provided in Your Word. Let me not become so content and comfortable in my place of well-being that I do not see those in need or hear their cries. Let me be aware of my environment and always seek for opportunities where I may be able to use my leadership, authority, and influence to make a difference. May my life always be a beacon of light, hope, and joy to all I meet. May You be glorified in me, and may I always extend my hand to those in need.

In Jesus' name, so let it be said. So let it be done. Amen.

AFFIRMATION

I am a cheerful giver.

I am kind to the poor.

I love my brother as myself.

I carry other's burdens and fulfill the law of Christ.

I do good and share with others.

I give to those who ask.

APPLICATION

Look for Opportunities to Make a Difference.

Think about how you might use your position of influence, your knowledge, skills, and resources to make a difference. As believers, it is important we do all that we are able, to impact and improve the lives of those who are poor or in need.

Write a personal impact statement. In this statement, identify what things you will do to make a difference, to be a beacon of hope and love for someone in need.

I will look for the signs and listen to the sounds of those in need (Proclamation).

I will work toward understanding the signs I receive and pray against. (Challenge or Opposition)

_____
_____
_____
_____
_____.

To overcome my challenges, I will (solution).

_____
_____.

 Overcoming Scripture: Write scriptures from the Word of God that you can have as a reminder when trusting the signs you receive from seeking your purpose and passion.

_____
_____
_____
_____.

Find a person who can be an accountability partner for you to help work on increasing your awareness and faith.

_____
_____

REFLECTIONS

Take a moment and write down your thoughts

_____

_____

_____

_____

_____

_____

_____

_____

_____

_____

_____

_____

_____

_____

_____

_____

_____

_____

_____

_____

_____

_____

_____

_____

_____

_____

_____

_____

ABOUT THE AUTHOR

LaWanna Bradford is a serial entrepreneur and global leader in the strategic planning and performance management arena. She is a thought leader and business management consultant who applies strategic thinking and business management concepts to maximize efficiency and effectiveness, and identify both business and life opportunities for improvement and growth. She is the COO of The Bradford Group, a commercial and investment mortgage brokerage and the Principal for The Bradford Group Consulting, a business management consulting firm. As a change agent, she leverages her 30+ years of experience working with federal and private industries and small businesses to guide individuals toward achieving growth, understanding their market position, and increasing awareness of the customers they serve. LaWanna is certified in Strategic Planning and Quality Management, and Georgia Oglethorpe Board Examiner's Training. She holds a Bachelor of Arts in Sociology from the University of Arizona, and a graduate degree in Administrative Organization and Management from Golden Gate University Graduate School of Public Administration. Her passion for shifting paradigms to encourage women to elevate to the highest versions of themselves is magnified in the Celebrate You Women Embracing Wellness movement, which she envisioned and co-founded. LaWanna is an international best-selling author, public speaker, trainer, philanthropist, artist, avid reader, and writer, who loves nature and spending time with her family. She believes life should be embraced in the moment of now and positive transformation and lasting empact in life and in business is achieved one strategy at a time.

CONTACT INFORMATION

Email Address: lawanna@bradfordgroupmtg.com

Website: https://www.bradfordgroupmtg.com

SOCIAL MEDIA

Twitter: @LaWannaBradford

Facebook Page: @lawanna.bradford.3

Facebook Business: @bradfordgroupmtg

Facebook Business: @bradfordgroupconsulting

LinkedIn: lawannabradford

RELEASE YOUR SOUND

Dr. Derashay Zorn

She opens her mouth with wisdom, And on her tongue is the law of kindness.
Proverbs 31:26

"Silence her!" Those are the words that ring in the thickness of the atmosphere from the executive boardrooms, political arenas, religious institutions, in homes, and the streets throughout the world, as if there is no value in the words that are released from the woman. They are not spoken out loud in some places. Yet, in others, they are very vocal, but in either case, the stench of it is ingrained in the minds and hearts of men and women alike. Statements are made very boldly through decisions that say, "I would not work, join, or support businesses, ministries, positions, and more because a woman leads it." Her capacity or capabilities to lead effectively are never considered. It's just another case of gender disparity. Therefore, many have worked hard to put women on mute without realizing they might be the ones who hold the solution to the problem they cannot solve. I can only imagine the impact and influence that could positively transform lives and save nations if they could take a moment and look beyond the fact that the one with the solution is a woman, if they would only allow her to release her sound, consider her thoughts, and enable her to operate in her wisdom, skills, and abilities unapologetically.

We commend women leaders who refused to be silent as they break up the status quo, raised above society dysfunctions, and released their sound. Their courage has laid the foundation and cracked open doors for many women to show up in their brilliance, unapologetically. Even with foundations laid and doors cracked open, there's still this glass ceiling that suppresses many women from releasing their sound. If it has ever been a time to break the glass divider and stand on the shoulders of those who have paved the way, indeed, the time is now. It is a time of awaking and activating the release of the sound that God has placed within you. Let's break the silence as Isaiah 52:1-3 is released upon us.

"Awake, awake, O Zion, clothe yourself with strength. Put on your garments of splendor, O Jerusalem, the holy city. The uncircumcised and defiled will not enter you again. Shake off your dust; rise up, sit enthroned, O Jerusalem. Free yourself from the chains on your neck, O

captive Daughter of Zion. For this is what the LORD says: 'You were sold for nothing, and without money, you will be redeemed,'" (**Isaiah 52:1-3**).

Release your sound transcends beyond the words you speak. It's the volume of your completeness and the impact of your mere existence. The word sound can be defined as complete, in good condition, not damaged, or diseased. The world needs you to operate in your *authentic self*, being fearfully and wonderfully made as it is written in Psalms 139:14. You can no longer show up playing small, living under the shadow of the imposter syndrome, nor dimming your light so that others can be comfortable. What is the sound that you should be making in the earth that will save lives, transform nations, set the captives free, and allow you to live freely in your skin? Let's take a journey in the lives of a few women and examine the difference in the impact and influence of deciding to be silent or moving beyond the barriers and releasing their sound

RELEASE YOUR SOUND TRANSCENDS BEYOND THE WORDS YOU SPEAK.

-DR. DERASHAY ZORN

The Proverbs 31 Woman must have understood that there was much power in releasing her sound. As we examine her life, it is evident her words spoke volumes in whatever hat she wore. In her business dealings, she had to communicate what she wanted and what she wasn't going to accept from her business operations to the negotiation tables. She had to take a stance and speak up not to be taken advantage of, and her brilliance with not being ignored or overlooked. Otherwise, her success would have been in the fate of men deciding to do the right things by her. She couldn't depend on that happening. Therefore, she had to have confidence in who she was and her capability and capacity to handle whatever business she handled. It was also evident that her husband expressed that same confidence as he didn't get involved in her affairs. I'm sure they discussed her ventures, and he trusted her abilities to start and manage them.

Unlike the Proverbs 31 woman, many women have been taken advantage of because they didn't feel comfortable enough to speak up even when they knew what was happening wasn't right. If she only had the confidence to lend her voice to the matter, she wouldn't have to leave the room feeling unsatisfied and underserved. The fear of speaking up due to the possible consequences have caused women to be vulnerable and at the disposal and discretion of a male governed society. Oh my, look at where the oppression of the woman's voice has gotten us. In the silence of anguish, women have had to watch businesses fail, religious institutions destroyed, political injustice prevailed, and lives utterly ruined because she dares not speak. It's time to speak up as society is collapsing right before our eyes because the answer is behind the mute of her voice.

I was among those who are muted until about 15 years ago. I didn't feel that my words had value as our society and my environment had drowned them out. My visions and dreams at that time were just memories that I considered would never happen. This falsehood was built through my life experiences, whether it was the childhood molestation that, if spoken, could have gotten me beat or the unresolved cry that I desired to finish high school while being a teenage mom. These things left me broken, uneducated, dreams shattered, and feeling like nothing of importance I said mattered. In anguish, I became mute, and life began to pass me with years of emptiness as I wanted to release my sound.

So, there was an awakening within me as I looked at my boys and desired more for my legacy than what life had handed me. I cried out to God as I knew that I had to be the one to change the trajectory of their lives. I didn't want these black males to be institutionalized prisoners, gang members, drug dealers, high school dropouts, teenage fathers, and the list can go on. This meant that I had to stand up and fight against everything that hindered me from releasing my sound. I had to become the difference and the change that I desired for them. That burning desire has taken me on a journey that I could not have imagined.

As I begin to make the sound for my legacy, this journey would take away the period behind my eighth-grade education and place commas for various degrees that included a Masters in Information Systems Technology with a Specialist in Database Design and a Doctorate in Theology. This path has led me into rooms that statistically I should not have been, in positions that my gender should have disqualified me, and places that men didn't accept me. But I stood and fought the good fight of faith because I know that I was making a sound to save nations.

When I decided to make a sound for my sons, I didn't realize that it was positioning me to become the lead outreach counselor at the Institute for Males, where I developed programs, systems and trained my team to help men develop personal, academic, and professional development plans. Yes, my sound became more significant than just my legacy as God expanded the passion for nations. I also recall being in a room full of Caucasian men as the only black and woman, and they tried to ignore my existence. They were working on a program that wouldn't work because of a syntax error. I solved the issue on the 1st day, but it was ignored. Therefore, it took three days and me mocking them before they would sarcastically decide to let me fix it. With the stroke of a few buttons, I had the program up and running. From that day forth, they had ears to hear my voice. Due to encounters such as these, God has entrusted me with entities such as the I AM H.E.R. International, media platforms, and other businesses alike to help others release their sound. Let's discover why you should be releasing your sound within the earth.

MAKE A SOUND TO UPHOLD YOUR DIGNITY

When women don't release their sound and stand up for what's right, we leave room for injustice to rise in our lives, and others are impacted negatively. Choosing to remain voiceless often diminishes our dignity. In the book of Genesis, when Sara kept silent and went along with the plot of just being Abram's sister when he was afraid, she jeopardized her life. Not speaking up for truth positioned her to be sexually abused, become an adulterer, become dishonored, and life took if she displeased the Pharaoh. Can you imagine Sara's mental and emotional state of being as Pharaoh decided to take her into his house? I can think of many things such as betrayed, abandon, worthless, rejected, unprotected, devalued, unloved, shamed, and more. It sounds pretty much like every woman who doesn't stand up for their rights.

> **NOTHING IS MORE VALUABLE THAN YOUR SELF-WORTH, NOT EVEN THE STATUS OF THE QUEEN.**
> **-DR. DERASHAY ZORN**

This decision didn't only impact Sara but also others. Her decision endangered innocent people's lives as plagues fell upon Pharaoh and his household. God had to intervene in this manner so that Abram and Sara could get back on track for His plans. This was unfortunate for Pharaoh's family, but it could have been prevented if she made a statement by stepping up for her rights not to be put in a position of such violation and defenselessness. She was the total opposite of Queen Vashti in the book of Esther. Vashti stood in her authority and demanded not to be the object of sexual exploitation.

Queen Vashti made a sound statement throughout the kingdom. She understood that nothing was more valuable than her self-worth, not even the status of the Queen. Her sound was so loud that they promptly decided to remove her as the Queen so that her statement would not influence other women to take the same stance as the Queen. Even though it was at the expense of her position, she was able to uphold her dignity.

Even in these times, women, *Queens,* are propositioned inappropriately to have a seat in the boardroom, advance in their careers, acquire contracts, go further in ministry, and even be a wife. These are defining moments when we have to stand in the soundness of our self-worth and refuse to compromise who we are for the sake of a position, title, or advancement Upholding your dignity is more valuable than anything man can ever give you. It's time to arise, women of God, and take the stand for righteousness. Also, when you understand God's purpose for your life, you will never have to compromise to obtain it. Make a covenant with God and yourself that you will uphold your dignity and not hold back on releasing your sound throughout the earth.

MAKE A SOUND AND LEAD NATIONS OUT OF CAPTIVITY

It is time for women to discover their sound and reign in their God-ordained position alongside our male counterparts to influence nations with their words positively. In the book of Judges, Deborah became an influencer to Israel's nation because she chose to step into her purpose unapologetically. I believe Deborah effectively served as Israel's leader in the prophet's office and judge because she understood her identity in the Lord. This woman didn't allow society to shape her identity. As she discovered who she was in God, she took ownership of her call and position despite how society functioned. It is evident in the response of the people to her leadership. It's worth noting that she is the only woman judge that is written about in the Bible. In addition, to serving as Israel's judge, she had wifely responsibilities.

This courageous woman served as a judge in a time when Israel was under the oppression of Canaan. She allowed God to use her voice so that they could be freed from their captivities. Look at how powerful her voice was to the nation. According to the word, the children of Israel came to Deborah for judgment. This means that her words held a lot of weight and influenced the lives of the Israelites. If her words were not significant, they would not have sought her to administrate judgment upon their matters.

YOUR SOUND IS GOING TO FREE NATIONS FROM CAPTIVITY

-DR. DERASHAY ZORN

We will also discover in the word the level of authority that this woman's voice carried that she called for Israel's army's commander Barak. When she called, he came to hear what she had to say and carried out her word so that Israel could be freed.

Women in leadership are not a new thing to God. He has called us to lead alongside our male counterparts despite their desires to silence us. We must not be silent because the freedom of nations hangs in the balance. I believe that as you discover and release your sound, it is going to impact nations. The moment you trust God, it will empower you to take ownership of your position. Only then will you discover that others will value your input in critical matters. You will also begin to recognize that the weight of what's in you has the ability to lead nations. Don't allow the magnitude of the assignment to overwhelm you, for it's in you to lead. I believe that our purpose is to deliver the promises of God to others. Now is the time to step into purpose and lead God's way within whatever atmosphere you are called. Nations are waiting to be led out of captivity, and your sound is the key to free them from their captive.

MAKE A SOUND FOR YOUR LEGACY

We are uniquely designed to leave legacies that will impact the lives of generations to come. However, legacies do not transpire without making a sound in the earth. It is developed by taking risks, making bold actions, defying the odds, overcoming fears, and the willingness to take on your God-ordained assignment. Women can no longer allow their visions, dreams, and brilliance to remain silent to accommodate those around them. We must begin to think about the impact of our silence. It's much greater than those who we are trying to make comfortable. There are lives that are at high risk of mental, emotional, spiritual, or physical death, poverty, or captivity.

In the book of Esther, the Jewish nation was at risk of being annihilated by the plot orchestrated by Haman. When Mordecai told Ester that she would have to go before the king and speak on behalf of the Jews so they would not die, his request was very risky for the Queen. It was custom that if anyone approached the king without being summoned, they were put to death instantly if he didn't hold out his scepter. Immediately, she resisted because she didn't feel that her life was worth the risk. The king had not made a request for her within the last thirty days.

"And Mordecai told *them* to answer Esther: "Do not think in your heart that you will escape in the king's palace any more than all the other Jews. For if you remain completely silent at this time, relief and deliverance will arise for the Jews from another place, but you and your father's house will perish. Yet who knows whether you have come to the kingdom for *such* a time as this?" *(Esther 4:13-14)*.

This response from Mordecai charged her, and it inspired her to leave a legacy that will change the lives of nations. We can take away the following from Queen Ester:

1. Don't waste another second to be invited to the tables of others. Make a mark, build your own, and they will come running to take a seat.

2. Overcome your fears of not being accepted by showing up in your authentic self. You'll be amazed who has been waiting on the true you.

3. Break the protocols, standards, and labels that have oppressed women within society. Some rules were made to be broken.

4. Take the risk. When you get on the other side, you are going to thank yourself for being brave.

5. Refuse to be silent because the sound that you need to make is significant enough to make a difference.

SUPPLICATION

Dear Father

You are magnificent and glorious in all your ways; there is truly no one like you. I give you honor and praise because you are the King of Glory. I thank you for being faithful to your word and preserving my life for the work in which you have established. You have declared that I am fearfully and wonderfully made, and I give you praise for your marvelous work. Therefore, I come before you asking, in the name of Jesus, for your healing and cleansing from every experience that I have encountered that has built beliefs that speak contrary to your word. Lord, help me break free from the barriers within my mind and the strongholds of the salience within society so that I may speak up for what's right and not consider the weight of society.

Oh Lord, I repent and ask for forgiveness for every time I should have spoken up, but I remained silent. I thank you for forgiving me for the iniquity of my sins and remembering them no more. As you have forgiven me, I now forgive myself for not speaking up and making a sound for what was right. I praise your name that I no longer have to be weighed down with the past, but I can advance freely within the truth of your Holy Word.

Today, I choose to make a stand in the truth of your words. I choose not to be silent and live behind the injustice of a society that mutes your voice in me. Fear will no longer keep me from opening my mouth. I declare that I shall open my mouth as you give me the utterance before men. No longer will I downplay that wisdom you have given me. I thank you today that the silence is broken. I thank you for the strength to no longer hold back my word and speak life among others. How I praise you that out of my belly shall flow rivers of living waters. I thank you that the words of my mouth and the meditation of my heart shall be acceptable unto you, oh Lord.

I thank you that my mouth shall feed the minds and the souls of nations. As I soak in your presence, I give you praise for giving me the words to speak and the heart to release them in the lives of others. You are truly thoughtful of me, and I cannot give you the praise that you deserve. Therefore, I will honor you with my life and do your work for my life, in the name of Jesus.

As the steps of the righteous are ordered by you, Lord, I trust you in every place you tread my feet upon, and I will obey you to release the sound that you have given unto me. I shall no longer be silent as I lift my voice and do that work unto you as an instrument for your glory. Thank you for entrusting me to deliver your words of wisdom in my home, in leadership, in ministry, in the marketplace, and the assembly of man. Your love is unfailing, and I am honored to be so loved by you. I thank you for a listening ear and a heart of concern. It is in the majestic name of Jesus that I pray. Amen.

AFFIRMATION

I am an amazing leader.

There is life in my words.

My words shall nourish the soul of others.

I shall speak life.

I shall make decisions with sound judgment.

I will not remain silent.

Out of my belly shall flow rivers of living water.

The wisdom upon my lips shall bless nations.

I have the wisdom to make sound business decisions.

My sound influences nations.

I operate from the soundness of my mind.

My wisdom shall be requested due to the soundness of my words.

Others will be positively impacted by my work.

I am fearfully and wonderfully made.

I am designed to do a good work.

I am tailormade.

I will not remain silent.

I shall do the work in which I was created.

I shall prosper in all my ways.

I shall uphold my dignity in all matters.

APPLICATION

D.A.R.E to Be YOU

Discover Your Sound – It is time to look beyond everything that has taken place in life and discover the impact of your sound.

What is your sound? How can it be utilized in the marketplace to impact the lives of others? If it's already in the marketplace, discover other platforms that could be used to leverage your sound.

_____

_____

_____

Activate Your Sound – There's no time for sitting on those gifts and holding back the treasures because others want to deny the power that resides within you. It's time for Operation Activate

Set a Date with Destiny and determine that date you will officially operate in your sound on a full-time or part-time status. Develop a plan on how you are going to begin your operations or expand into new territory.

_____

_____

_____

Release Your Sound – It's time to make some noise. The kind that gets noticed because of the influence and impacts your establishment will make.

Develop a visibility plan and market your brilliance. Press releases, branded content, interviews with intentional marketing, and cultivating relationship are your friends.

_____

_____

_____

Expand Your Sound – It's all about duplication so that your legacy is upheld. The sound that God has released in you is too great to be obtained in your city. Consider other ways that your sound can be released.

How can your sound be duplicated in other cities, states, and countries?

_____

_____

_____

REFLECTIONS

Take a moment and write down your thoughts

_____

_____

_____

_____

_____

_____

_____

_____

_____

_____

_____

_____

_____

_____

_____

_____

_____

_____

_____

_____

_____

_____

_____

_____

_____

_____

_____

_____

_____

ABOUT THE AUTHOR

Kingdom Strategist, Blueprint Builder, and Spiritual Midwife **Dr. Derashay Zorn** is an international business coach, best-selling author, and expert in the art of **unleashing purpose, developing dreams, and expanding untapped potentials within individuals, corporations, and ministries.** Her passion for information technology has led her to obtain a Master of Science in Information System Management, which equipped her to **specialize in analyzing, developing, and managing systems to birth or expand individuals and entities into the next dimension of kingdom implementation.**

Derashay equips mankind globally as the Founder of the **Kingdom Influencers Network, In The Church™ TV & Radio Broadcast, Divine Order Restoration Ministries (D.O.R.M) International, Kingdom Strategist Firm, Women of Influence Magazine, (D.O.R.M) Publishing,** and many other entrepreneurship endeavors that equip mankind globally. Through her global brands **Kingdom Strategies University® & Preneurs Academy®**, she teaches others **how to maximize their potential and monetize their gifts and talents** as a critical vehicle for fulfilling their purpose, making a significant impact, and branding influence that can instantly and beautifully change the world. Her books and workbook titled "**Abortions In the Church: Divine Strategies to Spiritual Deliverance,**" 31 Ways of Influence V1, & Meant for My Good: Being Developed In The Midst of the Disaster is helping others overcome and give birth to their purpose, visions, and dreams. She is a mother, pastor, entrepreneur, consultant, empowerment speaker, mentor, and friend.

Her philosophy is "**A critical tool for self-development is learning how to cultivate, build, and release others into their destinies.**"

CONTACT INFORMATION

Email Address: info@derashayzorn.com

Website: www.derashayzorn.com

SOCIAL MEDIA

Twitter: @kbstrategist

Facebook Page: @kingdomstrategist

Instagram: @kingdomstrategist

CONTACT DR. DERASHAY ZORN

FOR BOOKINGS

www.derashay.com or info@derashay.com

AVAILABLE TITLES

IF YOU ENJOYED THIS BOOK, HERE ARE OTHER DR. ZORN BOOKS AVAILABLE ON AMAZON:

Abortions In The Church: Divine Strategies to Spiritual Deliverance Book

Abortions In The Church: Divine Strategies to Spiritual Deliverance Workbook

Meant for My Good: Being Developed in the Midst of the Disaster Anthology

Parentpreneur Success Guide – Co-Author Edition

31 Ways of Influence Volume 1

UPCOMING PROJECTS

Delivering My Expectation

The Rules of Success

Influence 365 Devotional Anthology

40: The Wilderness Experience Survival Guide – Entrepreneurship Edition Anthology

I AM H.E.R. Collective Series Anthology

Meant for My Good Anthology V2

31 Ways of Influence V3 Anthology (2022)

Join Next Anthology by visiting https://px.fyi/imnextdrzorn